# Voice-Activated

*How to Discover Your Identity, Define Your Life, and Declare Your Future*

**BILL THEMELARAS**

*Voice-Activated* © 2021 by Bill Themelaras. All rights reserved.

Published by Author Academy Elite
PO Box 43, Powell, OH 43065
www.AuthorAcademyElite.com

All rights reserved. This book contains material protected under International and Federal Copyright Laws and Treaties. Any unauthorized reprint or use of this material is prohibited. No part of this book may be reproduced or transmitted in any form or by any means, electronic or mechanical, including photocopying, recording, or by any information storage and retrieval system, without express written permission from the author.

Identifiers:
Library of Congress Control Number: 2020921354
ISBN: 978-1-64746-584-1 (paperback)
ISBN: 978-1-64746-585-8 (hardback)
ISBN: 978-1-64746-586-5 (e-book)

Available in paperback, hardback, e-book, and audiobook

All Scripture quotations, unless otherwise indicated, are taken from the Holy Bible, New American Standard Bible®, NASB®. Copyright © 1960, 1962, 1963, 1968, 1971, 1972, 1973, 1975, 1977, 1995 by THE LOCKMAN FOUNDATION

A Corporation Not for Profit
LA HABRA, CA
All rights reserved worldwide.

Any Internet addresses (websites, blogs, etc.) and telephone numbers printed in this book are offered as a resource. They are not intended in any way to be or imply an endorsement by Author Academy Elite, nor does Author Academy Elite vouch for the content of these sites and numbers for the life of this book.

Some names and identifying details have been changed to protect the privacy of individuals.

## Dedication

To Lynne:
The first person I ever saw personally testify about Jesus.
The first person I ever heard pray in the Spirit.
The person who inspired me to pursue God.
My wife, lover, girlfriend, best friend, mother of my children, and my ministry partner.
I owe you everything.

# CONTENTS

## PART I
## WORDS

Chapter 1
Spirit and Sword

Chapter 2
Lawnmower Lessons

Chapter 3
God's Promises Are Voice-Activated

## PART II
## MOST PROBLEMS AND SOLUTIONS ARE IN THE UNSEEN WORLD

Chapter 4
Pray, Decree, and Declare

Chapter 5
A Full Pantry

## PART III
## THE FINISHED WORK OF CHRIST ON THE CROSS

Chapter 6
Discover Your Identity

Chapter 7
I Am

## PART IV
## IT'S TIME TO PRAY

Chapter 8
Inner Circle Prayers

Chapter 9
Outer Circle Prayers

## PART V
## MAKE IT PERSONAL

Chapter 10
Crafting Prayers

Chapter 11
Conclusion: The Challenge

# FOREWORD

*"Strength is for service, not for status."*
(Romans 15:1b, The Message)

*"For whatever was written in earlier times was written for our instruction, so that through perseverance and the encouragement of the Scriptures we might have hope."*
(Romans 15:4, NASB)

*"Good judgment depends mostly on experience and experience usually comes from poor judgment."* (Undetermined)

I think one of the most significant challenges most newcomers have when reading and obeying the Bible is the subtle error that allows them to dismiss its simplicity. God gave the nation of Israel Ten Commandments, the Jews expanded them to 613, and Jesus reduced them to two! *"The entire law and all the demands of the prophets are based on these two commandments."* (Matthew 22:40, NLT)

I am convinced of this fundamental principle I have learned: *The desire for simplicity is the process of an orderly mind.* Complex problems will eventually find simple answers.

When I am listening to or reading the words of gifted communicators, I invariably find specific attributes that are intrinsic to the experience. I am looking for an insight that I haven't had, or a fresh way of expressing an idea that resonates in my own soul, or even the novel use of a familiar word, I had not previously considered. I want to be "surprised," amused, enlightened, and even seeing something so plainly that it prompts me to say out loud, "Yeah, I knew that!" I have a friend who has a unique way of reducing the seeming complexity of an issue with unusual insight. I often want to use his expression and make it my own, and I have teasingly asked him, "Please help me put this in my own words."

The Bible is *the word of God*. Only a clear and unswerving commitment to this eternal principle will be the key to understanding how life works and recognizing that everything that God says is true. One of my mentors called it, "The Manufacturers Handbook." The Bible is a trusted account of the faith journey of God's people. Each writer is careful to include their successes and their failures, as well as their regrets and their rejoicings. It is an unedited, uncensored, and unredacted history of many of God's servants' fame and flaws. Our great heroes in these writings are never portrayed as unblemished in character, but we view each of them through the uncompromising lens of Scripture—warts and all.

And yet, the Bible is the unfolding story of the God of mercy and compassion, Who has the eternal desire to see us accomplish His unchanging purpose despite our frequent missteps. The Psalmist reminds us of this with these words, *"As parents feel for their children, God feels for those who fear him. He knows us inside and out, keeps in mind that we're made of mud."* (Psalm 103:13–14, The Message)

Pastor Bill Themelaras is an emerging apostolic leader in the body of Christ, whose love for God, for worship, and for God's word has forged in him a passion for seeing people become all they were created to be and do. Pastor Bill expresses this passion in his love for his amazing family. He oversees two thriving congregations, Oasis City Church in Columbus, OH, of which he and his wife, Lynne, are founding members. He is also my successor as the leader of Covenant Church of Pittsburgh, in Pittsburgh, PA. Both are dynamic, diverse, and growing families of worshippers. His sphere of apostolic leadership and oversight is expanding.

It has been my joy to serve as pastor, mentor, friend, and spiritual father to Bill and Lynne. A bonus and greater joy was when their three exceptional children, Nia, Cullen, and Skylar, chose to adopt my wife Barbara and me as grandparents. Pastor Bill's motivating principle in life is to be a worshipper; this is the one constant, foundational to everything else he does. Out of this fountainhead flows the other remarkable attributes I have seen mature and flower in his whole ministry. A five-tool player is a term used in baseball to describe an athlete who demonstrates competency, necessary skills to be a consummate world-class player. In the church, a gift mix containing creativity, administration, communication, wisdom, and prophetic insight seldom comes together in a single person. Still, when it does, it indicates a measure of responsibility that is forthcoming. It is said, "To whom much is given, much will be required."

Any consistent observation of a person's life will eventually yield significant insights into how that life is lived-out regarding their respect for words. Jesus admonished His disciples and others who would hear His teachings that they should exercise caution when using negative words to denigrate His teaching or his miracles. He solemnly warned them with these words: *"But I say to you that for every idle word men may speak, they will give an account of it in the day of judgment. For by your words, you will be justified, and by your words, you will be condemned."* (Matthew 12:36–37, NKJV)

This book is not the work of a theorist who is looking for captivating phrases for intellectual stimulation, but the result of the theorist who has to become the pragmatist who needs to be sure the principles and concepts actually work in real life and not just in the pastor's study or seminary. The writer of Hebrews describes the teacher who is willing to prove the truth of God's words when saying, *"But solid food is for the mature, for those who have their powers of discernment trained by constant practice to distinguish good from evil."* (Hebrews 5:14, ESV)

## Words Create Worlds

I believe the writer of Hebrews is declaring this in that mind-boggling passage in Hebrews 11:3, *"By faith we understand that the universe was created by the word of God, so that what is seen was not made out of things that are visible."* (Hebrews 11:3, ESV) Consider that persons created in the image of a creator are also creative! Many of us are very likely living happily or unhappily in a world that was "framed" by words we had spoken in the past. Idle words or careless words are not just phenomena; we quickly dismiss as though they are meaningless, but they are words that have the potential for death or life, and these kinds of words are uttered by hundreds of millions of people every hour of every day. This book is about the careful and judicious use of words and their inherent power to create worlds we will eventually hate or love.

Jacob's words, spoken in ignorance, released a word curse over his favorite wife, who died while giving birth to Benjamin (Genesis 35:18-19). Jacob had no idea that when he spoke these words to his father-in-law, Laban: *"Anyone* with whom you find your gods *shall not live."* Now Jacob did not know that Rachel had stolen her father's idol gods.

King David barely escaped his decree of death, over his own life, by his words spoken in ignorance and haste, when he judged the unknown perpetrator with these words. *"... and he said to Nathan, 'As the Lord lives, the man who has done this deserves to die'"* (2 Samuel 12:5, ESV). The operative word that spared him was "deserves." However, the fourfold restitution that he required took place in his own family, in the tragedies of the child's death, who was born to Bathsheba, the brutal sexual assault of his daughter, Tamar, by his son, and the betrayal and death of Absalom.

The Book of Ruth, however, depicts a captivating illustration of the power of words. In this story, we see that Ruth uses words to position her in the precise place to discover her destiny. Ruth uses words unknowingly to guide her to the exact spot where she meets Boaz, who happens to be God's answer to an unimaginably unthinkable future! When speaking to her future husband, Boaz, she still doesn't recognize the power of her words to her mother-in-law, when she asks, *"Why have I found favor in your sight that you should take notice of me, since I am a foreigner?"* (Ruth 2:10, NASB) If we return to the beginning of the narrative, it begins with these words, in 2:2. "And Ruth the Moabitess *said* to Naomi…" It is important to note that she expressed an intention and not just a desire. These are her very words in verses two and three. "Please let me go to *the* field and glean among the ears of grain after *one in whose sight I may find favor.*" And she said to her, "Go, my daughter." What follows is a desire expressed and even perhaps a decree that initiated a discovery of her true identity, a defining of her life purpose, and an inherent prophetic declaration of her future!

I believe that God's words to Jeremiah's complaint are words to be embraced and committed to a lifetime of stewardship. *"This is how God answered me: 'Take back those words, and I'll take you back. Then you'll stand tall before me. Use words truly and well. Don't stoop to cheap whining. Then, but only then, you'll speak for me. Let your words change them. Don't change your words to suit them.'"* (Jeremiah 15:19, The Message)

Pastor Bill gave birth to *Voice-Activated* through the matrix of living life as God intended it. It contains insights, lessons, examples, and encouragement to help every believer find his or her way through the maze of roads on to the "path of the just" that leads to life. I know that you will be inspired, encouraged, and enlarged in your walk with God through its principles.

Bishop Joseph L. Garlington, Sr.
Founding Pastor of Covenant Church of Pittsburgh
Presiding Bishop of Reconciliation! An International Network of Churches and Ministries®

# INTRODUCTION

Words are the primary way in which we communicate and have been used since the beginning of existence. God has used words for as long as human history has been recorded. I cannot imagine how God communicated in the vast expanse of eternity, but I know we have examples in chapter 1 of the book of Genesis in the Bible. The Godhead—Father, Son, and Holy Spirit—are described as working together in perfect unity from the beginning of this planet and throughout human history. Through spoken word, sign language, and written word, humans use language to express our thoughts. The spiritual realm also uses words to communicate and activate its plans and purposes, both good and evil. Tremendous power and opportunity come to us when our speech aligns with the Word of God and His intentions.

Throughout human history, God has communicated with humankind, using us as His mouthpiece. How would your life be different if aligned with God's will? What if you could pray in a manner that brought change to your current circumstances by using words that matter? Could changing your surroundings by giving language to your thoughts and desires align you with God's plan for your life?

I invite you on a brief journey to discover the power of words and prayer decrees to define areas of your life. My goal is to inspire you and provides means for you to arrive at a better future. Agreement with God's purpose is powerful and life-changing; I desire to live in all the fullness He provides. The years pass and bring all sorts of twists and turns, but God is faithful through it all. I believe He wants us to know

His plans and purposes so we can declare them. When we do this, we align ourselves and our surroundings with a powerful spiritual force. The will of God will begin to manifest, and when that happens, everything changes. We can live inspired to know and establish all that God has for us. Join me on this pathway to define your life through prayer.

# PART I

# WORDS

# CHAPTER 1

# SPIRIT AND SWORD

A man with a microphone once told this story:

"I got a nephew that works for the Shell oil company. About four years ago they moved him down to South America and I ain't seen him since. But he still thinks about my wife and me. Every Christmas he sends us a nice present. This past Christmas, he sent us a live bird. A green bird, had a little yellow top notch on his head, with some red feathers and a hooked beak. He sent this live bird to us all the way from Brazil. I tell ya something, that bird was delicious.

We had him for Christmas dinner. We fixed him with some dressin', cranberry sauce, and sweet potato casserole. Well, after Christmas, my nephew called, wanting to know if we got the bird. I said, 'We got him.' He wanted to know how we liked him, and I said, 'He was delicious.' He said, 'You don't mean you ate the bird?!' I said, 'Well, of course, we did.' My nephew got all upset and said, 'I paid a fortune for that bird! It could speak four languages.' I said, 'Well, he shoulda said something.'"

That joke has been around for decades and has been phrased in many different ways, but it always ends with the same point, "He should've said something."

Words are lifesaving. They are powerful and alive. They create and shape both your world and your worldview.

This book is about understanding how words can define your life. Whether or not you realize it, the words you speak may have already affected your current state in life. Once you grasp the multiple truths and the purpose of prayers and declarations, you will see a better future. This isn't merely positive confessions or solving a combination lock with your speech. It also does not tell you to focus only on having a positive mindset or applying life hacks from self-help books and videos. Learning the principles found in the Holy Scripture, understanding timeless truths, and implementing them with the guidance of the Holy Spirit helps you recognize you're not alone. The Lord partners with you, and as you walk with Him, your life unfolds in a new way. Your outlook changes, your relationships change—your life changes for the better.

From the very beginning, words created worlds and this truth is still alive today. What if you could reshape your life by making daily declarations that place you on a pathway to defining your future? When you learn the power of using words properly, you can discover a new world waiting for your arrival.

## Words are spirit

> *The Spirit alone gives eternal life. Human effort accomplishes nothing. And the very words I have spoken to you are spirit and life.* (John 6:63, NLT)

We must understand the spiritual nature of words.

Words are not only about language and communication. They have substance to them that is more than merely their literature meaning. The essence of words is spirit; they contain power and influence. When we recognize this essence, we unlock revelation and when we open revelation, we are given a new perspective. When we think with a renewed mind, our actions begin to change for the better, transforming our lives for good.

## Words are powerful

> *Death and life are in the power of the tongue,*
> *And those who love it will eat its fruit.* (Proverbs 18:21, NASB)

The Bible is full of references demonstrating this principle.

We are confronted with this phenomenon on every level of social involvement. Our society is constantly bombarded with videos, posts, images, and statements that either promote the building up or the tearing down of people. The scripture above mentions death before life. I feel this is because it's easier to speak death words rather than life words when we have unrenewed minds. In frustration, we easily veer into the negative lane of life and talk according to the challenges we are facing. In the problematic seasons, we must stay in the life-lane and speak those powerful life-giving words over our difficult situations.

> **The essence of words is spirit**

When we speak, we align ourselves with the life or death nature of the words we use.

## The devil is the father of lies

Lies seem to travel at the speed of light. Remember, the Father of lies masks himself as an angel of Light. Participating in gossip and slander puts you in agreement with the words of the enemy, and believing lies does the same. Guard your mind and heart against becoming one with the words that are evil at their core.

We have the choice to make our words life-giving.

Consider the meaning behind this instruction:

*Let no unwholesome word proceed from your mouth, but only such a word as is good for edification according to the need of the moment, so that it will give grace to those who hear. Do not grieve the Holy Spirit of God, by whom you were sealed for the day of redemption. Let all bitterness and wrath and anger and clamor and slander be put away from you, along with all malice. Be kind to one another, tender-hearted, forgiving each other, just as God in Christ also has forgiven you.* (Ephesians 4:29-32, NASB)

Words proceed—they move forward because they have energy. Holy Spirit instructs us not to speak any ugly or hateful words, but only words that lift up and encourage others. The next part of this passage implies that when we misuse words, we grieve the Holy Spirit. Imagine how He feels when His representatives on the Earth go against His very will and nature. Have you ever considered how He can grieve over our use of words? The next verse continues with which types of words we should refrain from, including insults, profanity, and the putting down of others.

Lastly, we are provided with the better option. We should be kind and tender-hearted when speaking to others and use words of forgiveness because we represent Christ. This is more than setting a good Christian example; it's about the benefits of quality relationships. The way we use our speech directly affects the quality of relationships we have with people.

## All words are spirit, but they are all not life

The book of Proverbs urges us to guard our hearts and everything that impacts life comes from the heart. Every one of us has been the victim and the perpetrator of using words the wrong way.

We can all agree gossip and slander are dangerous behaviors; back-biting and lying are things we never want to happen to us. This is evidence that not all words are life. They are all spirit, but we need to recognize which ones bring the proof of life.

*In the beginning was the Word, and the Word was with God, and the Word was God. He was in the beginning with God.* (John 1:1-2, NASB)

*And the Word became flesh, and dwelt among us, and we saw His glory, glory as of the only begotten from the Father, full of grace and truth.* (John 1:14, NASB)

In these scriptures, we learn an interesting truth about Jesus—He *is* the Word. He was there in the beginning and became flesh when He came to Earth in human form as a baby. Before this, He was spirit.

The scripture tells us that God is also a spirit. Genesis records all creation being brought about through the power of words. Those words were spoken in and by way of spirit. The spiritual components of words carry properties and energy that are more than audible sounds describing a moment or emotion. They contain a powerful, creative and definitive energy with them, forming both the immediate and the distant future. Imagine what happens when our word usage aligns with His, and the future we create when our words are in agreement with the revelatory Words of God.

## Words are swords

*His **speech** was smoother than butter,*
*But his heart was war;*
*His **words** were softer than oil,*
*Yet they **were drawn swords**.* (Psalm 55:21, NASB)

Why do we want words from God that are swords? Every day we face spiritual battles that require spiritual weapons of warfare.

> *And take the helmet of salvation, and the **sword** of the Spirit, which is the **word** of God.* (Ephesians 6:17, NASB)

> *in addition to all, taking up the shield of faith with which you will be able to extinguish all the **flaming arrows** of the evil one.* (Ephesians 6:16, NASB)

Have you ever been on the receiving end of an insult or been falsely accused? Or heard the angry complaints of another? These are examples of how words can be emotional flaming arrows. God provides a shield of faith for us to use in these spiritual battles.

The enemy attacks with words. Remember, he's the accuser!

An accuser uses words. A testimony uses words. Rejoicing uses words.

## An accuser uses words

We all choose how we speak and the intentions behind our word usage. When you accuse, you risk aligning yourself with the wrong side.

Accusation causes significant damage, especially if it's a false one, and this risk is not worthwhile. Even if the information you have is correct, there's a strong possibility you don't know the entire story. As a pastor, I've been the mediator in many relationship disputes and have the privilege of providing Godly counsel and care to people in similar situations. After all, getting along isn't always easy.

> An accuser uses words.
> A testimony uses words.
> Rejoicing uses words.

The sessions often start off the same way. One person lists their grievances, usually including several things that resulted in a disagreement or fight. That list gradually sounds a whole lot like an accusation, and it would be easy for any third party to agree with that accusation because of the way it's presented. It's not until I ask questions and listen to the other person's side of the story that the truth is found. It's been said, "There are three sides of a story: what you say happened, what I say happened, and what really happened." Blindly agreeing with an accusation puts you at risk of aligning with the enemy. Satan is called the accuser of the brethren and the father of lies. He loves when we make these mistakes and he capitalizes on them.

*The words of the reckless pierce like swords, but the tongue of the wise brings healing.* (Proverbs 12:18, NIV)

## Self-talk

I've listened to my *self-talk* and discovered that I don't live up to scriptural standards.

Have you ever stopped to listen to yourself? The way you speak to yourself in your mind? I've done this time and time again, even playing out entire hypothetical scenarios. While I often give others the benefit of the doubt, I rarely give it to myself. Maybe it's because I know how I think and what my tendencies are, but I tend to be harder on myself than others are towards me. Hearing that 70% of things we worry about don't actually happen made me realize I've wasted precious time and energy on hypothetical situations that didn't deserve my time and attention. My *self-talk* needed some help.

The way we talk about ourselves matters. The words we use to describe our circumstances are essential to the outcomes we experience and it is vital to know the heart of God on the matters at hand. When I'm confident in His word over a situation in my life, I'm able to speak accordingly and apply the scripture and revelation to my life directly. The way I talk about myself and to myself carries significant weight.

> **The way we talk about ourselves matters.**

*Let no unwholesome word proceed from your mouth, but only such a word as is good for edification **according to the need of the moment**, so that it will give grace to those who hear. Do not grieve the Holy Spirit of God, by whom you were sealed for the day of redemption.* (Ephesians 4:29-30, NASB)

## Resolve to guard your lips

Regard the presence of the Holy Spirit in your life. The Holy Spirit is a person who is grieved when we wound another person with our words. What if Jesus was sitting in the room when we say what we say? By the power and presence of the Holy Spirit, He is! The Holy Spirit lives in you, and He's not gossiping to you about others.

## Remove all words from your mouth that tear down others

When I look back on my life, I can remember arguments, accusations, praises, and encouragement that people said to me. I had no idea the impact they would have on me and how I would process life as I grew up. I wish I had known the power of those words at the time. I wish I had known how to use words to redefine my life and future. It's never too late to learn this lesson. Words are spirit and swords—they carry death and life.

## A testimony uses words

Words of testimony are lovely. They breed hope and faith and when others listen to them, they are encouraged. When we testify of the goodness of God and what He is doing in our lives, we bring tremendous encouragement to those listening. We overcome because of our testimony and the finished works of the cross.

> *And they overcame him because of the blood of the Lamb and because of the word of their testimony, and they did not love their life even when faced with death.* (Revelation 12:11, NASB)

## The power of the testimony

I'd much rather listen to testimonies than to complaints. When I hear others talk about the faithfulness of God, my faith increases. I begin to think hopeful thoughts and remember I serve a God who invades impossible situations. My life has been a journey of ups and downs, successes and failures, wounds and healings. I can imagine that yours feels the same. When at a low point, I surround myself with others who have had similar experiences or have helped others through similar circumstances. I love to hear how God showed Himself strong through the most disappointing seasons of life.

I listen to the encouraging words of others who can remind me that life isn't over; that God is not only with me right now, but He's also in my tomorrow. I begin to adjust my speech and testify to God's love and faithfulness to me. I remind myself and others what He's brought me through in the past, that He's with me in difficulty in the present, and He's also in my future. I'd rather speak testimonies than complaints.

## Rejoicing uses words

> *Rejoice in the Lord always; again I will say, rejoice!*
> (Philippians 4:4, NASB)

The Apostle Paul makes it very clear to the church—rejoice and keep rejoicing. The Bible is filled with examples of rejoicing. When we celebrate the Lord, we place our focus on Him and our attention turns towards His greatness and affection. Rejoicing can act as a sword against the enemy, reminding him that we serve a God who is bigger than the battles we may face. If you have a debilitating illness, think about the things you haven't been able to do. List them out, then expect to be able to do those things again. Talk to others about your plans. Don't rejoice only when the healing manifests, but rejoice now in your present circumstance because healing is yours.

Jesus has already borne your sickness and disease; he has carried your brokenness and pain. By His stripes, we have already been healed. If you've lost your job, are in a broken relationship or are having a conflict with family, are battling addiction, or having struggles with hopelessness—rejoice! This sounds like the opposite of what comes naturally, but that's why God instructs us to do so. It causes us to take our eyes off the problem and place them on God. Rejoice through your pain. It can become your testimony that you share with others when they are in a tumultuous time.

> *For as the rain comes down, and the snow from heaven,*
> *And do not return there,*
> *But water the earth,*
> *And make it bring forth and bud,*
> *That it may give seed to the sower*
> *And bread to the eater,*

> *So shall My word be that goes forth from My mouth;*
> *It shall not return to Me void,*
> *But it shall accomplish what I please,*
> *And it shall prosper in the thing for which I sent it.*
> (Isaiah 55:10-11, NKJV)

God doesn't allow His words to fall to the ground. His words accomplish exactly what pleases Him. They produce something that fulfills purpose and destiny. They are not empty or trite—they bring prosperity to things that were unsuccessful or barren. When we partner with the Word and apply it accordingly, it does the same in our lives. Our words won't return empty-handed. They help accomplish the will of God and bring life and prosperity to our future. When the Lord is with you, your words will not fall to the ground.

## Ground gained by prayer must be guarded through prayer

> *A man will be satisfied with good by the fruit of his words,*
> *And the deeds of a man's hands will return to him.*
> (Proverbs 12:14, NASB)

A man's words are like seeds—if they are wise and pure, they will bring forth the fruit accordingly. The good and encouraging words will bring life, not only to yourself, but to those around you. Your words are no different than your deeds; if the work of your hands can produce income, product or prosperity, then the same goes for the words of your mouth. They produce fruit for consumption. Your words provide life-giving calories to your daily life.

> **We have an extraordinary opportunity to partner with all of Heaven's resources when we align our voice to the scripture.**

Here's a promise: The fruit of your words brings good things to you. They are satisfying like a glass of cold water on a hot day.

> *The Lord has established His throne in the heavens,*
> *And His sovereignty rules over all.*
> *Bless the Lord, you His angels,*
> *Mighty in strength, who perform His word,*
> *Obeying the voice of His word!*
> *Bless the Lord, all you His hosts,*
> *You who serve Him, doing His will.* (Psalm 103:19-21, NASB)

> *Are not the angels all ministering spirits (servants) sent out in the service [of God for the assistance] of those who are to inherit salvation?* (Hebrews 1:14, AMP)

The angels give attention to His word and the VOICE of His word.

There are times that God declares a matter. The angels know their assignment and perform His word. Angels are ministering spirits who are sent to help us carry out the purpose of God. I believe there are times the angels are waiting for us to proclaim His word because they don't foresee the assignment until they hear it. They recognize if a declaration aligns with the word of God and act accordingly to perform it. An angelic audience is hearing our words and they minister to us. There isn't a shortage of divine power that can work on our behalf. We have an extraordinary opportunity to partner with all of Heaven's resources when we align our voice to the scripture. The scripture tells us when Daniel prayed and fasted for three weeks, the angel Gabriel appeared to him. Gabriel said, "…your words have been heard, and I have come because of your words." (Daniel 10:12, NASB)

The powerful truth is that Gabriel came to assist Daniel because of his words. Even if you cannot quote the scripture verse perfectly, angels can still come to your aid because our words activate heaven. It is not our ability to quote verses perfectly that releases God's power, but faith in His Word and His love for us. Faith is recognizable. One word from Him is enough to send our enemies running away. The powers of Heaven work on our behalf when we give voice to the Word of God.

God is always changing us, molding us into His image. His will is that our lives are transformed by having our minds renewed by His Word. It's a never-ending process while we are here on Earth. The fact of the matter is God wants to help us grow, and to make us into the likeness of Jesus. He also wants to do something through us.

Know the difference between what God wants to do to you and what He wants to do through you.

# CHAPTER 2

# LAWNMOWER LESSONS

In my early thirties, I faced a frustrating set of circumstances for my young family. My business partner and I had a small business that had about 25 employees. We were a hard-working bunch who provided a service to our community at several locations. It's challenging being a small business owner and employing a variety of people to work toward a common goal. Our small business became even more of a challenge when a business agreement went sour—what seemed like a good idea years prior turned into the most painful situation of my life. I was not only faced with decisions that would affect my family, but also those I was in business with and employed.

What I didn't consider at the time was the spiritual dynamic. I didn't think about spiritual forces that wanted to oppose me and anything that would make me prosperous. I didn't take into account those same forces could battle me, my partner, my family, and at the same time, consequentially affect those whom I employed. When demonic forces are at play, they don't care about collateral damage. After all, the enemy's job is to steal, kill, and destroy. In this season, I was allowed to see the spiritual side of a tough situation and learned the difference between battling people and battling spirits. It didn't necessarily make my life easier, but it did allow me the opportunity to grow spiritually, especially in the discipline of prayer.

As a teenager, my stepdad required a lot from me. He was a great man, a strong man, and a man who loved Jesus. But he was also a man who loved discipline, and this teenager was inclined to challenging authority. Don't get me wrong; I was a quality teenager. I loved Jesus and my parents, but I was learning how to respect authority because I came from a previously abusive home life. But now I had a new dad, so I was learning the rules and regulations of his household and it was a challenging time for me. Since I loved him and my mother, I knew I needed to make the best of it. Saying I disliked lawn work is an understatement, but I learned to accept physical labor and it helped me develop a strong work ethic.

I remembered the alone time I had while doing the lawn work as a teen and now years later I figured I could use that time to my advantage. I would learn to use that time to pray. I needed to grow in my prayer life if I was going to make it through this business challenge. I had an ancient lawnmower whose engine was deafening, but I could push it along knowing I could pray at the top of my voice and the roar of the mower would cover it up. This kept me from looking like a crazy neighbor. I would even mow the lawn before it needed to be done so I could be outdoors and pray with passion. I prayed in tongues and the Holy Spirit responded. I repeated what I heard and I realized the Holy Spirit was teaching me how to decree the intentions of His heart over my life. I felt empowered, my soul flooded with hope. I would also quote scripture and prayed those verses over my life. I realized I could make decrees and supplications even while doing other tasks. It was as though my spirit-man was awakened to another degree as I partnered with God's purposes.

My business struggle went on for over a year, but I continued to pray. There wasn't much else I could do because so many things were out of my control, but sometimes that's the best position to be in—without control. I was entirely dependent on the Lord and trusting Him through it all. I applied the many lessons I learned during those lawn mowing hours. I realized I could accomplish much in the spirit throughout my day.

Eventually I was praying all the time, whether under my breath or out loud. I could be in my car, in my office, at home, outdoors, or walking in the mall—almost everywhere. I can't say I didn't look suspect at times "talking to myself" in public. But I realized it was what I needed in life. I felt the burden to pray and I knew I had to accept the fact. I also enjoyed it, mainly because Holy Spirit was the Teacher. Even with regular prayer, my circumstances weren't changing. Yes, you read that correctly. I dedicated extensive time with the Lord in praying the Word, making decrees, hearing the Spirit, and feeling like I was making progress spiritually only to wake up each day to find myself in the same situation.

My life wasn't changing—my problems still existed. I still had the daily struggle of dealing with my situation. I had repented of making bad decisions and leadership mistakes, sought out professional advice, and cried on my wife's shoulder, hugging her and telling her I was afraid. At times, I struggled with anger and faced doubt. However, in my spirit, I could tell faith was rising. I was defining my life and declaring my future.

I couldn't put my finger on the exact reason, but I knew God would come through. I made up my mind that I was going to remain faithful in my walk with Jesus and learn everything I could through it all. I had moral support, counsel, and prayer from my spiritual father, Bishop Joseph Garlington. Close friends and family were there for me and I had a praying mom who I knew was petitioning Heaven on my behalf. I had a supportive wife who loved me through my failures and successes, and she wasn't giving up either.

She carried a quiet yet strong and stable faith. She always reminded me, "Everything is going to work out."

I determined to pursue God like never before, to use my prophecies as a weapon of spiritual warfare and not allow the enemy to intimidate me. I recognized my battle wasn't against a person, a system, or people. This battle was more spiritual than natural. Even though nothing seemed to change from day to day, I had to believe things were happening in the spirit. After more than a year of this life lesson, a "suddenly" occurred. It was over—the business challenge was settled and the struggle was finished. God showed up and His mercy and favor shined brightly. At that moment, I knew all the emotional and spiritual tension, the hours upon hours of prayer and the lessons from Heaven had paid off. I needed to go through it so I could change the course of my life.

> We can define our lives...by how we pray.

Life isn't easy; it's filled with surprises and opportunities to remain faithful and learn how to become a disciple of Jesus. Daily prayers and decrees will impact your reality. We can define our lives, not by the curveballs and disappointments of life, but by how we pray. Life is voice-activated.

## Hope is not deferred

My friend, Rob, has the gift of encouragement. As I was going through another challenging season of life, he would say to me, "Your hope is not deferred." After several weeks, his words resonated inside me and I began to believe it. God is faithful. It's His nature, and His faithfulness goes beyond my lifetime. He's been committed to every generation and I'm not exempt from it, even in the darkest period of my life.

I came to recognize that God is faithful and His promises were still true.

I encourage you to document and recall your hopes. What do you desire that hasn't yet come to pass? What new things can you still hope for in life? I believe we are to see and experience the fulfillment of His generational blessings upon the lives of His people. Bring your hopes back to mind from underneath your pillows, and once again place them before the Lord. Be aware of His promises.

*And now, Lord, what do I wait for and expect? My hope and expectation are in You.* (Psalm 39:7, AMP)

Allow your life to be an orchestration of His hope: past, present, and future. Believe your entire family tree will share in the results of fulfilled promises. Generational blessing and favor will flow because your hope is in the Lord, and that hope is not deferred. His promises are mightier than your mess and they will become your testimony. We can release prayers that bring structure into the chaos.

*The earth was without form and void, and darkness was over the face of the deep. And the Spirit of God was hovering over the face of the waters.* (Genesis 1:2, ESV)

Many scholars have written commentaries regarding the above verse and what the earth looked like at this point in time. The overarching theme from Genesis 1:2 is that the earth was chaos. It was formless, dark, and contained a vast expanse of waters. It had yet to receive the structure and life-forms God planned for it. Chaos abounded, but that did not intimidate God; after all, it was His creation. He had a larger, more elaborate plan. With the power of words, His creation was about to receive additional creations. With declarations, He created light and atmosphere, land and vegetation, stars and planets, and land and sea animals. He also brought about light, atmosphere, and humanity. There are things in creation we have yet to discover, and all this divine order came because of His voice.

When I was younger, I heard a preacher say, "When you have muscle, you move things by your hand. When you are filled with faith, you move things on command." I didn't understand the vastness of a statement like that. It's more than just two rhyming lines because it contains a powerful truth.

## When you want, you ask. When you have, you say.

Politeness is essential in my family. We teach our children that politely asking for things is much more kind than placing demands on others. When you're in a place of need, asking seems only appropriate—there's something about asking that keeps us humble. There's a principle of truth in the scripture stating if you ask, you will receive. We must recognize that God cares about our basic needs and He wants us to ask Him for that provision. After all, He is our Good Shepherd, and He provides all we need. There are dozens of scriptures demonstrating His goodness and provisions for His people; the Father enjoys meeting these needs.

There's another level of provision that should develop certainty and build confidence and that's when you realize what you already possess. What if Christians could recognize what they currently have as sons and daughters of the living God? When you understand what's in your possession, you can focus on using the power of that possession. You move your attention from what you don't have.

How foolish does it appear when we ask for things we already have? In this day and age, people understand the feeling of losing or forgetting a password and most websites have a link for a forgotten password. Forgetting the password does not nullify the truth that you have access to an account. However, there are steps that need to be taken in order to reset the password and activate the account. Sometimes your identity must be verified before access is granted. Many Christians have forgotten they have access to an account funded from the finished work of the cross.

If you have children, you can relate when your kids ask the same question multiple times until they grasp the truth. This is understandable when your child is learning during their elementary years. But if they continue asking the same basic questions throughout their teenage years or young adult years, it can be quite frustrating.

Something changed in our home when our children were able to make breakfast for themselves. As parents, a simple bowl of cereal made an impact on our Saturday mornings. After all, we purchased the bowls, the spoons, the cereal, and the milk. When our children were old enough to recognize they could pour for themselves, they didn't have to ask us to do it for them. When they asked us to do something they were more than capable of doing, we were able to point to the kitchen to prove we have already provided all they needed to make a sufficient breakfast. As the children grew older, the cereal turned into a full spread of breakfast items they were able to prepare.

When you realize what you possess in the storeroom of your life, there's a confidence and authority that builds within you. When you own something, you can use it to your advantage.

In our home, we value game nights. We find time throughout our busy schedules, some planned and others spontaneous, to spend time together as a family at home. Since we value game nights, we have games on hand that don't take a lot of preparation time. When we have the game in our possession, we can just pull it out and play, whether it's a board game, a card game, a video game, a lawn game or whatever. There are also times when we want to play something we haven't purchased yet. It can be quite frustrating as both a parent and a child being in a position of want.

If you have your own transportation, you can say, "I'm heading out for grocery shopping." When you don't have a vehicle, you need to ask for help to run errands. Yes, you could walk or take public transportation, but the point is if you didn't have access to those items, you would still need to ask for help. My teenage children have very busy calendars. School demands, church services and events, athletic schedules, and social functions can make it difficult to manage. These all require transportation of some sort and Lynne and I are responsible to make it happen. We jokingly say that at times it seems we are simply the taxi drivers in our children's worlds. I'm sure many parents can relate to this. Our children were constantly asking to be transported from place to place, since they had no means of their own. Now, even with drivers' licenses, they have to ask for use of the cars available for our busy family. At times the "wants" can seem quite demanding as the schedules collide. Even sharing vehicles can be difficult. Each of our children anticipate the day that they have their own vehicle, so they don't have to rely on asking for rides all the time. As a father, I very much enjoy providing for my children and I have throughout every stage of their lives. Of course, I rely on my wife daily because she's the one who really makes it all happen. Together, we have provided their needs. As our children have matured over the years, it's something special when they recognize they have access to use our provision to care for themselves.

There's a difference in having a driver's license and owning a car.

When I was 13 years old, I worked over the summer for a park system with a public pool. The law in West Virginia at the time was that you had to be 14 years of age to work. Because my mother was a friend of the manager at the pool, I was able to start a few months before I turned 14. I enjoyed working and earning a wage; I made $1.25 per hour when I began. That was a low wage then, and a ridiculously low one in today's standards, but every year my hourly wage would increase.

For the first couple of years I didn't have a driver's license, so I needed to ask for a ride to work for every shift. I wasn't forced to have a job; I wanted a job to earn money. To keep my job, I had to ask for help to get there. Years later, with another job, I was able to purchase a vehicle. At that point, I no longer needed to ask for transportation. Because I owned a car, I was able to drive myself every day I was scheduled to work. I was able to say to my parents, "I'm going to work today."

There are so many things you already have by the Spirit of God; you have access to the elements of Heaven even while you are on earth. Our Father has lavished us with every spiritual blessing from Heaven. We need to learn how to speak to circumstances from that perspective, rather than continually see ourselves in lack. You have supernatural access to things that can enrich your natural life.

> **In hope he believed against hope**

> *Every spiritual blessing in the heavenly realm has already been lavished upon us as a love gift from our wonderful heavenly Father, the Father of our Lord Jesus—all because he sees us wrapped into Christ. This is why we celebrate him with all our hearts!* (Ephesians 1:3, TPT)

> *That is why it depends on faith, in order that the promise may rest on grace and be guaranteed to all his offspring—not only to the adherent of the law but also to the one who shares the faith of Abraham, who is the Father of us all, as it is written, "I have made you the father of many nations"—in the presence of the God in whom he believed, who gives*

*life to the dead and calls into existence the things that do not exist. In hope he believed against hope, that he should become the Father of many nations, as he had been told, "So shall your offspring be." He did not weaken in faith when he considered his own body, which was as good as dead (since he was about a hundred years old), or when he considered the barrenness of Sarah's womb. No unbelief made him waver concerning the promise of God, but he grew strong in his faith as he gave glory to God, fully convinced that God was able to do what he had promised.* Romans (4:16-21, ESV)

Abraham continued to hope for something even though all odds were against it. Not only did it seem so unlikely that Sarah would conceive a child considering her history of barrenness, but also the fact that he was almost a hundred years old and she was ninety. There's a great contrast in hope alone and hope anchored in faith that God would do what He had promised. Without God there can be hope, but no true hope. As Christians, we hold to supernatural hope against the hope that the natural world provides. In reality, the only hope we have is the hope that God provides to us.

Consider the power of verse 17 in the context of this passage: as it is written, "I have made you the father of many nations"—in the presence of the God in whom he believed, who gives life to the dead and calls into existence the things that do not exist.

Our Heavenly Father is one who calls things into existence. As His sons and daughters, we can partner with Him in creating realities through prayers and declarations. Like Abraham, no unbelief will make us waver concerning the promises of God. Whatever He says we can possess, we can. Whatever He says is our inheritance, is, regardless of what we may be facing in the natural. When we are fully convinced, we pray with a different attitude, a different authority, and a different perspective.

Our words place a demand on a supply that's invisible; things we need in our current circumstances are available to us in the spirit. There's a supply available to us supernaturally, and one of the keys to open the access door is through our words. We must recognize the difference between wanting and having. Throughout life, we will be in situations of both. Jesus tells us to ask, so there's nothing wrong with doing so. Asking for things we need and desire are part of our absolute dependence on God.

# CHAPTER 3

# GOD'S PROMISES ARE VOICE-ACTIVATED

We love music and a fun atmosphere in our home. We have random dance parties that can pop up at any minute. Any night can turn into a dance party; we turn on the sound system and shout out songs and playlists. I'm thankful for voice-activated audio devices—it's exhilarating being alive with today's available technology. When we already own songs or pay for a subscription, we have access to a seemingly endless list of songs. All we have to do is say what we want, and it immediately begins to play in our home.

We like movie nights as well. And like music, we own many movies and have subscriptions to movie services that allow access to a library of thousands of films. Wanting to watch a film and finding out it's not available can be frustrating. We have voice-activated television capabilities, but sometimes we call out a phrase that isn't there. Speaking to something we don't have can be discouraging. As a parent, it puts me in a position to hear my children ask for something I can't give them. They are left wanting and frustrated, and I'm left investigating why the subscription I have cannot provide what we wanted. It's an entirely different feeling when we have the movie in the database. All we do is tell the application to play the film, then bam, it happens.

I love listening to music, singing, songwriting, and leading others in song. I play acoustic guitar, but I don't consider myself a guitarist. I never had proper lessons, and when I did make an attempt at lessons, I never followed through with them. I regret that but hope to discipline myself more in the future. This fact can create moments of frustration for me leading a song or practicing doing so. There are notes and chords I want to play and should play, but they are not in my toolbox of guitar skills. There are lead lines and melodies I hear correctly in my mind, but I cannot bring them into reality with my fingers. It leads me to say all sorts of things to both myself and fellow musicians, and they all basically sound the same, "I wish I could play...", "I want to...", "If I only had learned...", "Can you play this part..."

If I had the musical tools, I could access them when needed. If I had the skillset, I could even teach someone else how to play. Great producers know what needs to be performed and can explain it to the professional musicians.

Simply said:

When you want, you ask. When you have, you say.

## 30 day, 60 day, 180 day challenges

We've all seen the ever popular 30 day, 60 day, and 180 day or more challenges. They can be for diet, exercise, mental health, learning a new skill, creating better relationships and so on. They are advertised all over social media and we are encouraged to join a group and engage in the challenge. There's accountability, funny stories, and interesting statistics to see if these really work. Most of the time they do simply because they force you into a new habit that can ultimately turn into a new lifestyle. There are lot of books available and lots of money to be made on these types of self-improvement routines. I enjoy business so I can appreciate the process of creating a product that can help others, and in turn, financially provide for your family.

While taking care of our physical bodies is important, so is taking care of our soul and spirit. Emotional health is vital to our wellbeing and this is something I've learned a lot about recently, especially being married to Lynne. She is passionate about the subject and has spent years studying, teaching, and putting it into practice. Spiritual health is critical as well because we are spiritual beings. The relationship of our triune being is continually being discovered. Our mind, body, and spirit are intricately intertwined, and they all need our attention. When one part is failing or lacking it impacts the rest.

Sometimes it's easy to think our spiritual lives are complete through salvation in Jesus, coupled with worship and devotional reading of the Word. Add a few minutes of daily prayer and we are all set. Unfortunately, that's not the case because as disciples of Jesus we are on a continual pathway to growth. Getting to know Him and how He thinks about us is a beautiful discovery. We grow from simply drinking milk to eating the meat. The depths of worship in His presence are always being revealed to us if we are willing to seek Him. The Father is looking for people who will worship Him in spirit and in truth—it's a spiritual connection and prayer is a vital component. Declaring the scripture and God's intentions not only strengthens our spiritual lives, it makes a major impact on our surroundings. It also positively affects our soul and body in powerful ways.

As you continue reading, I'd like to offer you some challenges:

- What does your life look like if you accept a spiritual challenge?

- How does 30 days of praying for a specific topic impact you?
- What could the outcome be if you declared God's perspective in a few areas of your life for 60 days?
- Could your life be revolutionized if you had a dedicated approach to prayer for 180 days?

I believe the answer is an emphatic YES. I'll come back to this idea a little later in the book.

## Speaking in tongues

In the church, a variety of teachings exist on the subject of speaking in tongues. We should always examine the scripture, but not only in the light of our personal experience nor in the light of a particular denominational viewpoint. The Apostle Paul said we shouldn't be ignorant in spiritual gifts. One type of this gift is given to some for the benefit of the corporate body when the speaker addresses the congregation. This is a message spoken in tongues that requires an interpretation. When combined, this is congruent with prophecy. I've been used on both sides of this combination and it's a unique step of faith each time.

Another expression of the gift of tongues is speaking a foreign language you are not educated in. This is not necessarily prayer, but it's communication you deliver in a language not known naturally to you. Although I've not personally delivered that kind of tongue to my knowledge, I've been a witness to it. It's an amazing way to evangelize and to reach people of other ethnicities and educational studies by way of the spirit. Both of these examples are of tongues being used as a sign from God.

Since there are various types of tongues given as gifts, I want to be clear that I'm referring to our personal prayer language. This gift is provided to all believers as a devotional prayer language for the benefit of the individual who is speaking privately and directly to God. It's not a supernaturally given foreign language and it's not the prophetic message that needs an interpretation. It is our prayer language used by our spirit to pray in a direct manner in conjunction with the Holy Spirit. This is a gift of tongues available to all believers in Christ simply by asking for it.

> *Then what am I to do? I will pray with my spirit [by the Holy Spirit that is within me], but I will also pray [intelligently] with my mind and understanding; I will sing with my spirit [by the Holy Spirit that is within me], but I will sing [intelligently] with my mind and understanding also.* (1 Corinthians 14:15 AMP)

I see this scripture as having a twofold application. The first one is exactly how it reads, I pray both ways, with my spirit and with my mind. In my instance, I pray in the spirit (tongues) and with my mind (English) and understanding. When necessary, Holy Spirit will give you the interpretation of what you said in tongues. Then you can continue to pray by inspiration of the Holy Spirit with your spirit and with your mind. This is in your personal prayer time, when you learn the language of the Holy Spirit as He teaches us what we should continually pray for.

Secondly, there are areas of prayer and intercession that we cannot access without our heavenly prayer language. There is power in a perfect prayer because we are aligned with the Holy Spirit. This book isn't meant to be an expository on speaking in tongues or the baptism of the Holy Spirit. There are many great resources I can suggest on the subject.[1] The purpose is that you understand speaking in tongues is a gift. It's a spiritual language we have access to and once "unlocked," it radically changes our prayer life. This is an evidence of Holy Spirit baptism along with other examples of His power. It's a separate experience from the new birth of salvation and is available to all believers. When I was in my early 20's I read and listened to many of Kenneth Hagin's teachings on the Holy Spirit. One example he gave stated there is a difference between a well and a river, though both contain water. A well is likened to eternal salvation when we drink of the living water of Jesus.

> *Jesus answered and said to her, "If you knew the gift of God, and who it is who says to you, 'Give Me a drink,' you would have asked Him, and He would have given you living water."*
> (John 4:10, NASB)

> *Jesus answered and said to her, "Everyone who drinks of this water will thirst again; but whoever drinks of the water that I will give him shall never thirst; but the water that I will give him will become in him a well of water springing up to eternal life."* (John 4:13-14, NASB)

Jesus is talking about receiving eternal life. He spoke to Nicodemus in the same manner. In the work of salvation, the well of the Holy Spirit is opened to us for everlasting life.

---

[1] *Seventy Reasons For Speaking in Tongues* by Dr. Bill Hamon
*The Bible Way to Receive the Holy Spirit* by Kenneth E. Hagin
*The Hidden Power of Speaking in Tongues* by Mahesh Chavda
*Tongues: Beyond the Upper Room* by Kenneth E. Hagin
*The Beauty of Spiritual Language* by Jack Hayford

There's another expression Jesus mentioned:

> *Now on the last day, the great day of the feast, Jesus stood and cried out, saying, "If anyone is thirsty, let him come to Me and drink. "He who believes in Me, as the Scripture said, 'From his innermost being will flow rivers of living water.' " But this He spoke of the Spirit, whom those who believed in Him were to receive; for the Spirit was not yet given, because Jesus was not yet glorified.* (John 7:37-39, NASB)

Jesus said rivers of living water will flow from inside of us. Not just one river, but multiple rivers. There is water in a well, and there is water in a river. The water in essence is the same, but the water in the well serves one purpose and the water in the river is for another. Both of these examples represent the Holy Spirit, and Jesus is telling us there are two experiences. One is to receive eternal life and the other enables God's power to flow out of you to bless other people. Both are gifts from God to His children.

Many scriptures throughout the Book of Acts exemplify the baptism in the Holy Spirit and the occurrence of speaking in tongues. Many of them also include prophecy. People would be baptized in the Holy Spirit, speak in tongues, and prophesy. There are different types of speaking in tongues and they all serve a purpose; the truth is we receive a language to communicate in prayer. When using this language, it's as if we enter into a super-charged prayer life. We can receive the gift of the Holy Spirit as quickly and easily as we received the gift of salvation. That is a wonderful and life-changing promise. It's not a matter of seeking out the gift of tongues, but of seeking the giver—the Holy Spirit.

We can expect to receive our prayer language because the Bible provides evidence of receiving Him in His fullness. Because we live in a voice-activated spiritual realm, the action of speaking in tongues is important. The examples in the Book of Acts and other areas in the New Testament show that to pray in the Spirit, we must speak. We need to open our mouths because speaking and giving voice to the gift of tongues is how we function in our new prayer language. Jesus also invites us to be filled with the Holy Spirit. How do we get filled with water? By drinking. Jesus invites us to "come and drink." This can also be compared to speaking freely in tongues until our spirit is satisfied. The Apostle Paul writes about that as well in the scripture below.

> Because we live in a voice-activated spiritual realm, the action of speaking in tongues is important.

*For by one Spirit we were all baptized into one body, whether Jews or Greeks, whether slaves or free, and we were all made to drink of one Spirit.* (1 Corinthians 12:13, NASB)

We drink of the Spirit and every person is designed in this manner. Not only are we created to do this, it's clear we all drink from the same Holy Spirit. Just because we drink water doesn't mean we are full of water. In the same way, it's one experience to be born again by the Spirit, and another to be filled with the Spirit. There is no option of being partially filled. Keep drinking.

*For one who speaks in a tongue does not speak to men but to God; for no one understands, but in his spirit he speaks mysteries.* (1 Corinthians 14:2, NASB)

The Holy Spirit will speak through us when we speak in tongues. We may even speak mysteries, things we don't understand but He does. It's a supernatural means of speaking to God. We need both kinds of prayer, meaning praying with the spirit and praying with understanding. While this book is written to teach about declaring the scripture and

God's purposes, please understand we also need to be praying in tongues. It cannot be one or the other. Holy Spirit doesn't pray apart from us, He helps us pray when we do the speaking. Remember, Holy Spirit is our Helper and our Teacher.

> *In the same way the Spirit also helps our weakness; for we do not know how to pray as we should, but the Spirit Himself intercedes for us with groanings too deep for words; and He who searches the hearts knows what the mind of the Spirit is, because He intercedes for the saints according to the will of God.* (Romans 8:26-27, NASB)

One of the reasons I love to pray in tongues is that it keeps me aware of His indwelling presence, stimulating my faith.

> *But you, beloved, building yourselves up on your most holy faith, praying in the Holy Spirit,* (Jude 20, NASB)

We all need our faith to be continually built up; there's a strengthening that comes by entering into this type of prayer. I recommend you add praying in tongues to your daily discipline of other prayers, which we will discuss in the next section.

# PART II

# MOST PROBLEMS AND SOLUTIONS ARE IN THE UNSEEN WORLD

# CHAPTER 4

# PRAY, DECREE, AND DECLARE

I want to provide some clarity and descriptions for prayers, decrees, and declarations as they are similar, but each have a distinct purpose.

The Merriam-Webster Dictionary defines these words this way:

pray (v)
    1. to request or plea
    2. to address God or a god with adoration, confession, supplication or thanksgiving

decree (n)
    1. an order usually having the force of law
    2. a religious ordinance enacted by council or head
    3. a judicial decision

decree (v)
    1. to command
    2. to determine or order judicially

declaration (n)
    1. the act of declaring
    2. a statement made by a party to a legal transaction
    3. something that is declared

Prayer is the dialogue between God and His covenant people and is found throughout the scriptures. Jesus displayed an active, regular, and intense life of prayer. Declarations and decrees are types of prayer, and when we understand the authority we have in partnership with God, we can be fully active in re-shaping our world. Declarations are spiritually powerful as we speak into the atmosphere what we already possess in the Kingdom of God. Decrees are tools we use that cause God's Kingdom and will to manifest on earth, just as it is in Heaven. It manifests heavenly realms to our natural realm so we can walk in that reality. We decree healing when we are sick because we know it's already been purchased for us through the finished work of the cross. We decree provision when we face lack because we already know it's God's will to fully satisfy every need we have.

Jesus showed that God provides for the birds of the air, and He loves His children much more than them; therefore, He will provide for us. We can decree peace when we are surrounded by storms of life. A decree carries authority from the King. When we decree God's blessings, we say that anything purposed against them cannot remain in our lives. Those decrees only have dominion when they align with God's desires, which is why it's best to do so according to the scripture. Decreeing our own desire or vision apart from the heart of God causes confusion and frustration.

Declarations are used to make known a truth, an accounting to a matter at hand. If you've ever traveled internationally, you had to go through Customs. An agent will typically ask you the question, "Do you have anything to declare?" If so, you need to account for everything you are bringing into the country. In the spiritual sense, we declare what we possess. We make known to our atmosphere that through Jesus, we carry the authority of heaven. We can combat every circumstance we face that battles the purpose of God in our life. We can declare the victory we have through Jesus Christ.

*He who dwells in the secret place of the Most High*
*Shall abide under the shadow of the Almighty.*
*I will say of the Lord, "He is my refuge and my fortress;*
*My God, in Him I will trust."*
*Surely He shall deliver you from the snare of the fowler*
*And from the perilous pestilence.*
*He shall cover you with His feathers,*
*And under His wings you shall take refuge;*
*His truth shall be your shield and buckler.*
(Psalm 91:1-4, NKJV)

There is so much to unpack in just the first two verses. God is giving us a glimpse of Himself and what we have access to because of who He is. First, He tells us He is the Most High. It is the Hebrew word, "Elyon," which means supreme monarch; the One who is elevated above all things; the Majestic One. This describes who owns the secret place and we are under the Most High. He is the supreme King of all and is elevated above all things in the universe.

Then He tells us that He is Almighty, which means El Shaddai, mighty and powerful; the One who supplies. We can abide in the shadow of the most powerful One

> **We make known to our atmosphere that through Jesus, we carry the authority of heaven.**

who has always been and always will be. From His position of might, He provides everything we need. There are future needs we are unaware of now, and He is still the One who will supply everything. He overshadows us with His strength and His provision, meaning we don't have to go anywhere else for security.

In Verse 2, He is identified as Lord, YHWH, which is the personal name for God that was revealed to Moses at the burning bush. He's the personal God to the people, the divine Ruler of their lives. And finally, in the same sentence, we see the fourth description with the words, "My God." This is the word Elohim, which means Creator. It's the name used in Genesis 1:1 and includes the creative power of the Godhead: Father, Son, and Holy Spirit. We are encouraged to trust in the master creator of all things. These four terms are vital to our prayer lives so we realize Who is covering us, and that God wants us to recognize the extreme benefits we have when we dwell with Him. Our prayers adjust according to Who is listening.

Verse 2 "I will say…"

What if portions of the deliverance and protection described after Verse 2 are activated by what we say? What happens in our lives when we say God is our refuge and our fortress? Will we trust Him no matter what? All sorts of His protection are revealed to us when we make simple declarations of His truth and dominion in the earth. We have access to God, who is Elyon, El Shaddai, YHWH, and Elohim.

As New Covenant believers, we can think differently than those when this text was written because of our knowledge of what came after. Imagine the servants of God of old seeking out the secret place, reading and hearing this passage and longing to be there. Maybe they thought only prophets and priests could enter this place. For us, the secret has been revealed and we have admission to the doorway.

How do you find it? This is where Jesus dwells. Since we are seated with Him in Heavenly places, we have entry right now. The Psalmist was prophesying and seeing himself with the Lord, but this is now our daily reality.

> "You will pray to Him, and He will hear you;
> And you will pay your vows.
> "You will also decree a thing, and it will be established for you;
> And Light will shine on your ways. (Job 22:27-28, NASB)

The word *decree* means to command, ordain, or decide. There's a difference in praying for something and declaring something with authority here on the earth. God promises to hear our prayers, and He also answers our prayers. In the same manner, he allows his children to take dominion in the affairs of our world. It is great trust when Holy Spirit desires to partner with us on the earth; however, we must know what decrees can be made that align with His will.

We get a glimpse of the power of praying and decreeing in Job 22. We see in Verse 28 that three things happen in accordance with one another. First, we have to speak up and decree something to our current circumstances so it becomes established for us. Why? Because the unseen world then aligns with the truth of God's heart. Just as we read earlier, angels give attention to the voice of His word. As we declare the Word of God over our lives and situations, there's a stirring in the spirit realm and angelic help is on the way. Our words through declarations become established when they line up with the intentions of God's heart and our surroundings change. Things in the natural realm and the supernatural realm come into divine order.

Once this happens, Light will come and shine on our ways. No longer would darkness and uncertainty have dominion in our lives. They must surrender to the power of Light. This trifecta is potent—decree something, it's established, then Light comes. The responsibility to know what to decree and how to do it is upon us. The spiritual truth of the power of declaration comes as a discovered gemstone on the pathway of life.

> **This trifecta is potent—decree something, it's established, then Light comes.**

The key to understanding what to declare is getting to know the heart of God and how He thinks, how He feels, what He says, and what He has already said. We are responsible as ambassadors of God's Kingdom to make righteous declarations over the earth and the world's system we face daily.

There's a fascinating example of the power of words and a decree in the scripture. Let's look first at this passage:

> *Now the men of the city said to Elisha, "Behold, the situation of this city is pleasant, as my lord sees, but the water is bad, and the land is unfruitful." He said, "Bring me a new bowl, and put salt in it." So they brought it to him. Then he went to the spring of water and threw salt in it and said, "Thus says the Lord, I have healed this water; from now on neither death nor miscarriage shall come from it." So the water has been healed to this day, according to the word that Elisha spoke.* (2 Kings 2:19-22, ESV)

We read that Jericho's men came to Elisha and told him how much trouble the city was having. For 500 years, the water was bad and the land was unfruitful. The women had battled miscarriages and babies died prematurely. Can you imagine living in a place like that and the stories passed down through the generations of the disappointment and trauma that would come from living under those circumstances? It had been happening for so long that the people were accustomed to it and had no dreams of change.

When Elisha came to that land as he was assigned, the people brought a great warning to him. There were even prophets living near Jericho who may have brought hope to those in the city. Unfortunately, none of them had the influence or the instruction on how to change the living conditions of the land until Elisha came. In the previous chapter, we read that he picked up Elijah's mantle and was on a mission. He was walking in a double portion anointing but hadn't had the opportunity to function in it. We saw that

Elisha would heal the water, which brought healing to the land and to the mothers' ability to deliver healthy babies.

This miracle was a game-changer for the city of Jericho. Part of that miracle was the concept of a salt covenant. The other piece was Elisha knowing what he needed to decree as he heard the Lord and deliver the declaration that carried with it the power of Heaven. With his obedience in placing the salt in the water, a prophetic action, and in using his voice to decree the word of the Lord, there came great healing. The waters were made pure for future generations.

Now let's take a look at what happened 500 years earlier that cursed the city of Jericho. It's found in the book of Joshua.

> *Joshua laid an oath on them at that time, saying, "Cursed before the Lord be the man who rises up and rebuilds this city, Jericho. "At the cost of his firstborn shall he lay its foundation, and at the cost of his youngest son shall he set up its gates."* (Joshua 6:26, ESV)

Jericho was an impressive and fortified city whose citizens worshipped false gods. By way of a tremendous miracle of obedience and faith, the city's walls came down, and Israel won a great victory. Joshua clearly didn't want it to be rebuilt, nor for the people to turn back to false gods, so he had made an oath over the land and cursed it. This curse was proven to be true many years later during the reign of King Ahab.

> *And Ahab made an Asherah. Ahab did more to provoke the Lord, the God of Israel, to anger than all the kings of Israel who were before him. In his days Hiel of Bethel built Jericho. He laid its foundation at the cost of Abiram his firstborn, and set up its gates at the cost of his youngest son Segub, according to the word of the Lord, which he spoke by Joshua the son of Nun.* (1 Kings 16:33-34, ESV)

Either no one told Hiel of Joshua's curse, or he didn't believe it if they did. Hiel lost both his firstborn son and his youngest son when rebuilding Jericho. There is no explanation why he continued with the building project after losing his first son, but again, maybe he was unaware of the oath. Perhaps the prospect of high financial gain had clouded his ability to see what was happening. The word about what Joshua had declared was likely circulating, yet Hiel was acting in defiance. He tried to rebuild a city God said He would judge. Over 500 years had passed, but Joshua's word was still being upheld over the land.

By the time Elisha came along, the curse had not only been spoken, but had taken action and was still active. A principle we can learn from this is when a word is spoken as a decree, it doesn't have a time-value; it goes on and on. It can only be canceled when a word of higher authority comes to break the curse.

Because the waters were made pure, they served as confirmation the decree worked. There was tangible evidence that God's word, when spoken, changed the course of an entire city and its future inhabitants.

I can imagine you saying to yourself, "But that was Elisha. That was Joshua. How can I relate to those powerful men of God?" Keep reading to learn how God wants to partner with you as well.

# CHAPTER 5

# A FULL PANTRY

I prefer having a full pantry. Maybe it's because I grew up in poverty. My parents lived paycheck to paycheck and always struggled to have an abundance of food in the house. Our needs were met, but we lacked in amount, variety, and diversity of food. Some payday Fridays were an exception because my mom would treat us with take-out, a pizza delivery, or a fast-food restaurant visit. I looked forward to those special days. Whenever I could, I would save coins that would add up to dollars so I could buy treats for my friends and myself.

When I was a teenager, I visited a friend's house one day, and his mother asked what we wanted for lunch. She listed items she could make for us, and I can remember thinking, "What? They have all of that food here, right now?" I was immediately taken back to years prior when I volunteered at a local grocery store. It was a small corner store on a street filled with a few bars, a produce market, and an apartment building. My mother's friend was the manager, so we would stop in often for them to chat. I found myself helping organize the shelves. I would stock the sliding glass coolers with bottles and cans of soda, making sure the label was properly facing forward and that everything was aligned correctly. I enjoyed seeing the shelves filled with supply in an orderly fashion so customers could easily find items. My mom's friend would reward me with a bakery item, candy bar, or soda.

I was happy to help with making the store look fully stocked. The one thing that bothered me was seeing the scarcely stocked shelves and realizing the store had replacement products just sitting in the storage room. I thought it would be best if the boxes in storage were unpacked so the customers could see the place was full. As an adult, I'm still the same way. I love having an organized pantry full of a variety of items that can handle most of our family's appetite. I like having a menu idea and the means to immediately produce it. Life should be like that too.

What if we believed that heaven was stocked full of all the items we need in life and we understood that our Heavenly Father would supply our daily needs? What if our faith wasn't in our socioeconomic status, but we wholeheartedly believed God is our source?

If you want something in your life, call it. If you want something out of your life, send it.

## Ungodly beliefs

I've learned great truths from Dr. Chester and Betsy Kylstra, the founders of Restoring the Foundations International. They teach a unique, integrated approach to healing and deliverance ministry. Their instruction and revelation regarding "ungodly beliefs" has been life-changing for me. We all have beliefs about ourselves and life, and when these beliefs conflict with God's truth, they are considered to be ungodly beliefs. All of us have formed ungodly beliefs from life experiences, including beliefs we've inherited generationally. They are lies that we believe about ourselves, about others, and ultimately about God. They affect our perceptions, our actions, and our daily life. These beliefs need to be changed into "Godly beliefs" through repentance and renewing the mind. There is great freedom and power in living with a belief system that's filled with the truth and accuracy of the Scripture.

## Belief System

> *If you sow a Belief*
> *You reap a Thought.*
> *If you sow a Thought*
> *You reap an Attitude.*
> *If you sow an Attitude*
> *You reap an Action.*
> *If you sow an Action*
> *You reap a Habit.*
> *If you sow a Habit*
> *You reap a Character.*
> *If you sow a Character*
> *You reap a Destiny.*
> (Author Unknown)

Ungodly beliefs can provide legal grounds and permission for demonic oppression in our lives. This happens as we come into agreement with the powers of darkness, rather than with the power of God in certain areas of our lives.

> *All praise to God, the Father of our Lord Jesus Christ, who has blessed us with every spiritual blessing in the heavenly realms because we are united with Christ.* (Ephesians 1:3 NLT)

You are not the exception. Every spiritual blessing is yours.

You are chosen to be holy and blameless. You are chosen as an adopted child. There's an identity shift from being an orphan to becoming an adopted child. You can look at yourself in the mirror and declare this truth.

God isn't angry at you. He's not looking for your sin; He's looking at you through the blood of Jesus Christ. Jesus took your sin upon Himself so that you could be blameless in the sight of God.

Take a moment and say those words over yourself:

Every spiritual blessing is mine.
I am chosen to be holy and blameless. I am chosen as an adopted child. There's an identity shift taking me from being an orphan to becoming an adopted child. God isn't angry at me. He's not looking for my sin; He's looking at me through the blood of Jesus Christ. Jesus took my sin upon Himself so that I could be blameless in the sight of God.
I am a son of God. I am a daughter of God. (whichever applies)
I am holy and blameless in God's sight, not by my works but because of what Jesus did for me.
I will walk in victory.
I am forgiven and cleansed from my mistakes, as if I had never sinned.
I am loved unconditionally.

What happens in our daily life when we begin making declarations that sound like that?

The enemy wants to use our old identity against us. He whispers into our mind with words about our past to hold us in the bondage of sin through the stronghold of our mind. Demons want to convince us that even though we are saved, we were never set completely free through Jesus. They want us to believe the lie that though we've repented from our sin, we'll never truly escape our previous lifestyles.

> **Don't be a death parrot!**

We can become our own worst enemies by placing our identity in the mistakes we've made. When we think negative thoughts and say negative words about ourselves, we give ammunition to the enemy. Demons love to join in the chorus of the words in our brain. Most often, the enemy speaks to you in the first person. He plants thoughts in our minds like, "I will never…this always happens to me…I can't…" When we repeat these words, we become the enemy's parrot.

Here are some trick thoughts from the powers of darkness:

- I'll never change.
- I'm not set free.
- This doesn't work for me.
- This is too hard.
- Reading the Bible doesn't work for me.
- Prayer doesn't work for me.
- I'm disqualified because of my past.

Ultimately, these are words of death. Don't be a death parrot!

These lies are ungodly beliefs, and when we give in to them, not only are we sinning, but we're also creating a pattern of defeat. This cycle will become a destructive force in our lives. When we believe these lies, even though they may feel real, we are giving in to demons and their thought processes.

Renew your mind with who God says you are. It's an incredible exchange—we give God all of our negativity, dark thoughts, and lies, and in turn, He gives us freedom and peace. The God of peace is with us and His peace isn't wimpy or passive. His peace is active and aggressive. Yes, it's an aggressive peace; one that has the power to calm raging storms, trample on darkness, disrupt opposing strategies, and break through opposing forces. It's real in both the spirit and natural realms.

## Dr. Masaru Emoto's water experiment

Dr. Emoto was an internationally renowned Japanese scientist who discovered water can carry information and can express that information to the world. He studied water for over twenty years, wrote books, and provided research and lectures to the science world. His book *The Hidden Messages in Water* was a New York Times Bestseller. His study showed that words, regardless of language or intention, have a physical impact on water. His research allowed others to see it through the photography of crystallized water molecules. He froze water and studied it under a microscope; as the water melted, it made crystal forms. These forms would vary based upon audible words spoken to them. He studied the scientific evidence of how the molecular structure in water transforms when it is exposed to human words, thoughts, sounds, and intentions.

He discovered the molecules of water were affected by positive or negative words and expressions. The water exposed to negative vibrations didn't always form crystals, but when it did, they were deformed shapes. However, the water exposed to positive things such as beautiful music, positive words, or prayer, tended to create beautiful, sometimes symmetrical, crystal forms. The vibration of words has such an impact on the listener. Since humans are composed mostly of water, his discovery shows how much impact positive words can have on our physical health. I don't know much about Dr. Emoto's spiritual life or if he accepted Christ before he died. He often mentioned the Creator and believed that God has placed a secret in water to prove the positive power of harmony and the words we use. He has been criticized by some commentators and scientists, as most theories are.

Science continually proves the existence of a Creator, and of a master plan imbedded in all of creation. It discovers the complexities of human life, the animal kingdom, the earth and all its dynamics. There is so much to learn about the mind of God and His design of the world we know, let alone the vast expanse of the universe. Dr. Emoto's research showed that words had a physical impact on water. The stunning beauty of the crystals formed from the simple words of "love" and "gratitude" are remarkable, no matter which language they are spoken in. Negative words like "you fool" or "you make me sick," or even songs with lyrics about heartbreak or death created twisted or ugly crystal formations.

> **Is it possible that your physical body has been affected by negative words spoken over you?**

Water makes up 70 percent of our bodies. Is it possible that your physical body has been affected by negative words spoken over you? Have you spoken words that could be making an impact on your health, or allowed a toxic atmosphere into your home or workplace that is taking a toll on you? If so, it's not too late to reverse these problems. My goal is to provide enlightenment on this subject and give you keys to transform your world.

## Storms and trials

> *So be truly glad. There is wonderful joy ahead, even though you must endure many trials for a little while. These trials will show that your faith is genuine. It is being tested as fire tests and purifies gold—though your faith is far more precious than mere gold. So when your faith remains strong through*

*many trials, it will bring you much praise and glory and honor on the day when Jesus Christ is revealed to the whole world.* (1 Peter 1:6-7, NLT)

Happiness can be dependent on the circumstance at hand, but joy is rooted in our soul. As Christians, our experiences of joy and hope are not defined by the moment. They are independent of our current surroundings because they're centered in what we know to be true about God and His Kingdom. Joy is a spiritual reality and something we have access to even in our most difficult times. Even storms and trials can be occasions to express joy because it is the trampoline of life—you can bounce back.

Storms don't last a lifetime, but our faith needs to remain strong through it all. When this happens, Jesus is glorified. The goal in our testing, as metals are purified by fire, is the proof of our genuine faith and character. Our faith turns everything we believe, our doctrine, into practice. This kind of faith and living hope can enable us to rejoice even when we are called to suffer grief in trials. We have overcome the world because of Christ.

There are many examples of these types of storms in the scriptures. Some are sent by God for a specific purpose and some are the product of evil spirits attacking the people of God. Both physical storms and emotional storms affect us. Unavoidable internal and external challenges can hit as storms of bad news, grief, and illness. Even the disciples in the boat with Jesus didn't know what to do when the storm came. Some of them were trained fishermen who were familiar with the raging storms on the Sea of Galilee. They fished on it most of their lives and knew how to read the clouds and the wind, but they were surprised by what happened. The scripture describes it as coming on suddenly and fiercely.

## A Full Pantry

*Then Jesus got into the boat and started across the lake with his disciples. Suddenly, a fierce storm struck the lake, with waves breaking into the boat. But Jesus was sleeping. The disciples went and woke him up, shouting, "Lord, save us! We're going to drown!"*

*Jesus responded, "Why are you afraid? You have so little faith!" Then he got up and rebuked the wind and waves, and suddenly there was a great calm.* (Matthew 8:23-26, NLT)

Was this solely a natural event or did it have a spiritual component? Could the enemy fashion a storm to take the boat by surprise and bring an end to the lives on board? Certainly, this would take out the Messiah and His messengers. But Jesus wasn't afraid nor was He impressed by the storm. Before He determined to deal with the weather, He rebuked His own disciples for their lack of faith. Their faith was the important factor because it had the opportunity to either get them through the external events or let them fall victim to it.

They had an emotional storm to battle as well, and this was fear. They were afraid, even though Jesus was there with them, especially since He was sleeping. They ran to wake Him and shouted for Him to do something. It was evident they had more faith in the storm destroying them than they did in God's ability to see them through it. Mark's Gospel reads, "Teacher, don't you care that we're going to drown?" They were uncertain of Jesus' motives and questioned His concern for them.

Jesus was on a mission to go to the other side. He knew that the Father was with Him, so He was able to rest. This wasn't a typical night's sleep; it was a sleep so deep

> **Three words changed everything.**

that He slept through the raging winds, rain and waves. The

boat was rocking violently through it all, and there was Jesus, fast asleep. Mark's Gospel also tells us what Jesus did in His rebuke of the storm.

> *And he awoke and rebuked the wind and said to the sea, "Peace! Be still!" And the wind ceased, and there was a great calm.* (Mark 4:39 ESV)

"Peace! Be still!"

Three words changed everything. Jesus spoke to the storm and took authority over it through His words. Could the disciples have done this as well, or was He only successful because He was the Son of God? Could it be another example of our words, when aligned with the purpose of God, having major impact on our surroundings? Remember, they were on a mission to get to the other side. They had a Heavenly assignment, and something was trying to prevent it from being completed. Jesus used this incident to show His power and to expose the fear and lack of faith of His own disciples. He made this a teaching moment they would never forget, and He gave them a key to face battles that would come in the future.

Take a look at how Paul describes his circumstances:

> *Three times I was beaten with rods. Once I was stoned. Three times I was shipwrecked. Once I spent a whole night and a day adrift at sea. I have traveled on many long journeys. I have faced danger from rivers and from robbers. I have faced danger from my own people, the Jews, as well as from the Gentiles. I have faced danger in the cities, in the deserts, and on the seas. And I have faced danger from men who claim to be believers but are not. I have worked hard and long, enduring many sleepless nights. I have been hungry and thirsty and have often gone without food. I have shivered in the cold,*

*without enough clothing to keep me warm.* (2 Corinthians 11:25-27, NLT)

This life experience was challenging, but we know Jesus was with Paul through all of it. Paul surely prayed through these incidents. It wasn't easy to endure these circumstances and some of these dangers lasted for weeks at a time. This is the same Paul who also told us to rejoice in times of trouble, just as he did while imprisoned for the sake of the Gospel. It's obvious God used these difficulties for His glory in Paul's life and in the early church. The book of Acts is filled with examples of trials and persecutions, dangers and sufferings. Miracles, signs and wonders are also prevalent. The tension lies in understanding how God uses it all and how we can learn to partner with His plan and purpose within our circumstances. Prayer opened prison doors, set captives free, healed the lame, raised the dead, shook buildings, cast out demons, and empowered Christians to do the work of the ministry. These are just a few instances written in Acts and may they be an inspiration and example today.

There are plenty of books written and sermons preached on trials and tribulations. My goal is to encourage us to have an influence on our surroundings with words. We must know the difference between the storms that God causes and the storms of the enemy. If God hasn't created it for His purposes, then mankind has the authority to rebuke it. Lesser authority is always subject to a higher authority. We have the power through the Holy Spirit to pray against all the demonic storms the enemy tosses our way, both individually and collectively.

# PART III

# THE FINISHED WORK OF CHRIST ON THE CROSS

# CHAPTER 6

# DISCOVER YOUR IDENTITY

Soon I will present "Inner Circle" and "Outer Circle" prayers that you can declare over your life. First, I'd like to discuss our identity as believers in Jesus Christ. It's critical you renew your mind with the truth of the finished work of the cross and who you are now as a new creation in Jesus. I recommend making these identity statements daily, weekly, and monthly until they become entirely real to you. It's always good to read them, allow the truth to process in your spirit and soul, and repeat them anytime you feel the need. I have prepared a list of "I Am Decrees" to help you on this journey. It's not an exhaustive list, but it does cover many common areas of life.

Part of what I included is a simple list you can decree, and the other part shows supporting scripture for each statement. Take your time to study the statement with the supporting scripture and allow it to sink deep in your heart. Don't be in a hurry to rush through the list. The important things are that these identity statements become part of you, and you have an understanding of them. Life and the enemy will throw many circumstances your way that will try to challenge these truths. When you know who you are in Christ, an abundance of authority is released. You can declare these statements and scripture with pure revelation as your mind and soul are convinced of their truth.

As my dear friends Georgian and Winnie Banov have taught for many years, the Bible teaches that we are joined with Christ in several areas. The prefix "co" closes the gap. There is no distance between you and Jesus. This shows the closest possible union you and I could have with Him. Peer into the ultimate truth revealed in these scriptures:

*We were buried therefore with Him by the baptism into death, so that just as Christ was raised from the dead by the glorious [power] of the Father, so we too might [habitually] live and behave in newness of life.*

*For if we have become one with Him by sharing a death like His, we shall also be [one with Him in sharing] His resurrection [by a new life lived for God].* (Romans 6:4-5, AMP)

*And if we are [His] children, then we are [His] heirs also: heirs of God and fellow heirs with Christ [sharing His inheritance with Him]; only we must share His suffering if we are to share His glory.* (Romans 8:17, AMP)

*And He raised us up together with Him and made us sit down together [giving us joint seating with Him] in the heavenly sphere [by virtue of our being] in Christ Jesus (the Messiah, the Anointed One).* (Ephesians 2:6, AMP)

We share so much with Jesus and only by His amazing grace. Because of the finished work of the cross, we are joined with Him not only in His suffering, but also in His glory. We are joined in the crucifixion, burial, and resurrection of Jesus. We are seated with Him in Heavenly places and are His joint heirs for everything the Father has for His Son. Our natural and carnal minds resist this mind-blowing truth, so we must renew our minds to the absolute truth of God's Word. This is why Jesus refers to Holy Spirit as the Spirit of Truth that will guide and teach us.

It's imperative we understand this so we can walk in the absolute authority and freedom given to us as believers in Jesus. Our minds must be renewed in order to think and live in the authority provided for us. Demonic forces want nothing more than to keep us from understanding our rights and authority. The world's system is structured contrary to the Kingdom of God. Religious systems also resist this truth as they resisted Jesus as the Messiah. When we declare these truths, we are no longer enslaved to the religious order. No longer are we submissive to the system of the world because we can worship and live in the freedom of all Jesus accomplished on our behalf.

We are:

Co-Crucified with Christ
Co-Buried with Christ
Co-Resurrected with Christ
Co-Glorified with Christ
Co-Seated in Heaven with Christ
Co-Heirs with Christ

Therefore, we can apply these truths to renew our minds:

- I live from a New Covenant
- I live with a purpose
- I am in union with Christ
- My old identity is dead
- The stronghold of sin has been dismantled within me
- I am dead to sin once and for all
- I am perfectly righteous because of Christ
- I have God's grace (His empowering presence)
- I live by faith
- I live in communion with Holy Spirit and not from a list of rules

- I am a (son or daughter) who knows God as my Father
- I have permanent access to a perfect relationship with God
- I overflow with hope
- I am at peace with God
- I overflow with joy
- I am empowered to walk in new life
- I am robed with God's power
- I live together in God's triumphant power
- I walk by faith and not by sight
- I am seated with Christ in Heaven right now
- I can share in all the treasures of Jesus
- I inherit all that Jesus is, and all Jesus has
- I have been co-glorified with Christ; therefore, the fullness of the Godhead lives in me
- I am an ambassador of Jesus in this world
- I am free – entirely and wonderfully free

This is our identity as believers in Jesus Christ! It's critical that we continually renew our minds with the truth of the finished work of Christ on the cross.

## Sleep

You can make declarations over your sleep. The traditional view from scripture states your day begins with sundown. It comes from the wording found in Genesis.

> *And there was evening, and there was morning—the first day.* (Genesis 1:5, NIV)

> *And there was evening, and there was morning—the second day.* (Genesis 1:8, NIV)

It's important to discover God's order and His systems. When we gain understanding and put them into practice, we can reap certain benefits. As you follow the system, you earn the rewards of that system. What if the battles you face throughout the day could be won the night before? What would your life look like if you were victorious while you slept? The freshness of a morning filled with victory will set a new tone throughout your day. Tomorrow begins at sundown tonight.

You've probably heard the phrase "sleep on it." We don't know where this idiom originated, but we all know what it means. When faced with a tough choice, it's best to take time, pray, and give it a day or two after resting before making a decision. As Christians, we can also ask God to instruct us at night while we are sleeping. The Holy Spirit can deposit new ideas and wisdom overnight, giving us tools for us the next day.

It's good to prepare ourselves before we sleep by turning off entertainment and taking time to pray. Bless your own mind and soul to rest and hear the voice of God so you can go to bed with your affections on the Holy Spirit. He wants to own the night and have us awaken with His refreshing Presence each morning.

*In a dream, a vision of the night,*
*When sound sleep falls on men,*
*While they slumber in their beds,*
*Then He opens the ears of men,*
*And seals their instruction,* (Job 33:15-16, NASB)

In our sleep, He seals our instruction. This is remarkable. Even when we are consciously unaware, He can open our ears and speak to us while we rest. He provides dreams, but the enemy wants to disrupt this process with fear and anxiety to hinder us from hearing the Lord. Imagine how great it would feel going to bed knowing you will encounter God, even if you don't remember it the next morning. He seals our instruction so the next day we can walk in the wisdom of God we received the night before.

> *The way you counsel and correct me makes me praise you more, for your whispers in the night give me wisdom, showing me what to do next.* (Psalm 16:7, TPT)

The above passage is further evidence these nighttime encounters can be transformational. Take a moment to thank Him for whispering to you tonight and for showing you the steps to make each day. He wants to use your sleep to show you what to do next. Imagine the battles He fights on our behalf when we are unaware!

I especially love Psalm 127:2 in The Passion Translation. It provides powerful insight into how God views our efforts and His provision. Each time I'm challenged in the area of finance and provision, I'm reminded of this verse. The last line speaks to me and increases my faith every time.

> *It really is senseless to work so hard from early morning till late at night, toiling to make a living for fear of not having enough. God can provide for his lovers even while they sleep!*

## Prophecy

Another crucial factor in our prayer life is prophecy. I have extensive experience in learning and teaching the prophetic. The more I learn, the more I realize I don't know, but it's undoubtedly a fun journey with the Lord. Prophetic process encompasses a lot, and while that's not what this book is about, it should be briefly addressed. When we understand the intentions of God's heart through prophecy, we gain confidence in who we are in Christ.

Prophecies are weapons. Use them to your advantage.

You can learn to use your prophecies as weapons to fight on your behalf. When declaring your prophecies, you are stating what God says He will do in your life. They become mighty forces to not only renew your mind with the truth, but also to war with the powers of darkness assigned to torment you.

> **When declaring your prophecies, you are stating what God says He will do in your life.**

We can be frustrated when previous prophetic words have not yet come to pass. Especially when you see no possible way for it to happen, don't allow yourself to stay in a position of doubt by burying that prophetic word under a pile of papers on your desk. A prophecy is a promise! When you give voice to that promise in your prayer life, you are welcoming Heaven's assistance. After all, the angels know the voice, and God can assign them to minister to us. We come into agreement with Holy Spirit when we pray His promises over our lives.

> *So Timothy, my son, I am entrusting you with this responsibility, in keeping with the very first prophecies that were spoken over your life, and are now in the process of fulfillment in this great work of ministry, in keeping with the prophecies spoken over you. With this encouragement, use your prophecies as weapons as you wage spiritual warfare by faith and with a clean conscience. For there are many who reject these virtues and are now destitute of the true faith,* (1 Tim 1:18-19, TPT)
>
> *This command I entrust to you, Timothy, my son, in accordance with the prophecies previously made concerning you, that by them you fight the good fight, keeping faith and a good*

*conscience, which some have rejected and suffered shipwreck in regard to their faith.* (1 Tim 1:18-19, NASB)

I love both of these translations of this scripture. Our prior prophecies should be taken seriously enough that they become weapons of our spiritual warfare. We literally fight the good fight by faith. It's our responsibility to keep these prophetic words, review them, and pray with them. It's also true that prophecy needs to be judged and examined. This is why you need the spiritual input of a pastor or leader in your life. All prophecy is potential. It's conditional and not just a list of absolutes. God is speaking to potential in our lives and contains a sometimes hidden "if," meaning it can be conditional on other things God is speaking and our obedience to Him. We can pull the favor, authority, and influence of who God says we are into our current identity. It's our responsibility to find the conditions and commands within the word. This is where we do our part and can take personal responsibility in obedience and prayer.

I encourage you to write the prophecies spoken over you and continue listening to them. A simple way to understand them is by highlighting specific sentences with two colors. Choose one color to highlight the things God said He would do, and another color to highlight the things you are supposed to do. For the latter, find the conditions or commands God addresses. This is where you can accelerate the word to come to pass. We must do our part by acting on the instructions as soon as possible. Search the prophecy for any statements that speak about your identity, then circle or underline them so you can see and speak who God says you are. You can pull the favor, authority, and influence of who heaven says you are into your current season.

It's vital you agree with God. When this happens, tremendous spiritual force is created that you can use as a weapon in battle. Your prophecy is a useful weapon in the good fight of faith.

You may be asking, "But what if I don't have a personal prophecy? No one has ever given me a prophetic word." Don't be discouraged because there are over 5,000 promises in the scripture. As I mentioned, a prophecy is a promise, therefore you can grab hold of those promises in the Word of God for your life. Ask the Father to reveal some of the promises He wants you to focus on, then use them to fight through the spiritual obstacles in life. You can define your future by declaring personal prophecies and the promises of scripture over your life.

# CHAPTER 7

# I AM

It's vital we use the scripture in our prayer life. When we combine praying in the Spirit with declaring God's Word, we enter an empowered experience. Below is a list of "I Am Decrees," along with supporting scripture references. These truths define who we are in Christ. Read them, pray them, feed on them, drink from them, mediate over them, and decree these certainties from Heaven.

## I Am Decrees

I am born again.
*Jesus answered and said to him, "Truly, truly, I say to you, unless one is born again he cannot see the kingdom of God."* (John 3:3, NASB)

I am a new creation.
*Therefore if anyone is in Christ, he is a new creature; the old things passed away; behold, new things have come.* (2 Corinthians 5:17, NASB)

I am forgiven.
*Who pardons all your iniquities, Who heals all your diseases;* (Psalm 103:3, NASB)

# I Am

I am called.
*So all the peoples of the earth will see that you are called by the name of the Lord, and they will be afraid of you.* (Deuteronomy 28:10, NASB)

I am strong.
*Finally, be strong in the Lord and in the strength of His might.* (Ephesians 6:10, NASB)

I am healed.
*and He Himself bore our sins in His body on the cross, so that we might die to sin and live to righteousness; for by His wounds you were healed.* (1 Peter 2:24, NASB)

I am whole.
*Now may the God of peace Himself sanctify you entirely; and may your spirit and soul and body be preserved complete, without blame at the coming of our Lord Jesus Christ.* (1 Thessalonians 5:23, NASB)

I am a healer.
*Heal the sick, raise the dead, cleanse the lepers, cast out demons. Freely you received, freely give.* (Matthew 10:8, NASB)

I am a giver.
*Give, and it will be given to you. They will pour into your lap a good measure—pressed down, shaken together, and running over. For by your standard of measure it will be measured to you in return.* (Luke 6:38, NASB)

I am the future.
*You did not choose Me but I chose you, and appointed you that you would go and bear fruit, and that your fruit would remain, so that whatever you ask of the Father in My name He may give to you.* (John 15:16, NASB)

I am destiny.
*Before I formed you in the womb I knew you, And before you were born I consecrated you; I have appointed you a prophet to the nations.* (Jeremiah 1:5, NASB)

I am wonderfully made.
*I will give thanks to You, for I am fearfully and wonderfully made; Wonderful are Your works, And my soul knows it very well.* (Psalm 139:14, NASB)

I am rich.
*For you know the grace of our Lord Jesus Christ, that though He was rich, yet for your sake He became poor, so that you through His poverty might become rich.* (2 Corinthians 8:9, NASB)

I am wisdom.
*But by His doing you are in Christ Jesus, who became to us wisdom from God, and righteousness and sanctification, and redemption,* (I Corinthians 1:30, NASB)

I am understanding.
*We are from God; he who knows God listens to us; he who is not from God does not listen to us. By this we know the spirit of truth and the spirit of error.* (1 John 4:6, NASB)

I am revelation knowledge.
*that the God of our Lord Jesus Christ, the Father of glory, may give to you a spirit of wisdom and of revelation in the knowledge of Him.* (Ephesians 1:17, NASB)

I am patience.
*strengthened with all power, according to His glorious might, for the attaining of all steadfastness and patience; joyously giving thanks to the Father, who has qualified us to share in*

*the inheritance of the saints in Light.* (Colossians 1:11-12, NASB)

I am endurance.
*strengthened with all power, according to His glorious might, for the attaining of all steadfastness and patience; joyously giving thanks to the Father, who has qualified us to share in the inheritance of the saints in Light.* (Colossians 1:11-12, NASB)

I am a miracle.
*Heal the sick, raise the dead, cleanse the lepers, cast out demons. Freely you received, freely give.* (Matthew 10:8, NASB)

I am a wonder.
*while You extend Your hand to heal, and signs and wonders take place through the name of Your holy servant Jesus.* (Acts 4:30, NASB)

I am a sign.
*while You extend Your hand to heal, and signs and wonders take place through the name of Your holy servant Jesus.* (Acts 4:30, NASB)

I am good news.
*How lovely on the mountains are the feet of him who brings good news, who announces peace and brings good news of happiness, who announces salvation, and says to Zion, "Your God reigns!"* (Isaiah 52:7, NASB)

I am a treasure.
*For the Lord has chosen Jacob for Himself, Israel for His own possession.* (Psalm 135:4, NASB)

I am the apple of His eye.
*For thus says the Lord of hosts, "After glory He has sent Me against the nations which plunder you, for he who touches you, touches the apple of His eye."* (Zechariah 2:8, NASB)

I am peace.
*Now may the Lord of peace Himself continually grant you peace in every circumstance. The Lord be with you all!* (2 Thessalonians 3:16, NASB)

I am obedient.
*All these blessings will come upon you and overtake you if you obey the Lord your God...* (Deuteronomy 28:2, NASB)

I am faithful.
*He who is faithful in a very little thing is faithful also in much; and he who is unrighteous in a very little thing is unrighteous also in much.* (Luke 16:10, NASB)

I am truthful.
*Be diligent to present yourself approved to God as a workman who does not need to be ashamed, accurately handling the word of truth.* (2 Timothy 2:15, NASB)

I am perseverant.
*Not that I have already obtained it or have already become perfect, but I press on so that I may lay hold of that for which also I was laid hold of by Christ Jesus.*
(Philippians 3:12, NASB)

I am grace.
*And God is able to make all grace abound to you, so that always having all sufficiency in everything, you may have an abundance for every good deed;* (2 Corinthians 9:8, NASB)

## I Am

I am mercy.
*Be merciful, just as your Father is merciful.*
(Luke 6:36, NASB)

I am justified.
*So then as through one transgression there resulted condemnation to all men, even so through one act of righteousness there resulted justification of life to all men.*
(Romans 5:18, NASB)

I am provision.
*I will abundantly bless her provision; I will satisfy her needy with bread.* (Psalm 132:15, NASB)

I am prosperity.
*Honor the Lord from your wealth
And from the first of all your produce; so your barns will be filled with plenty and your vats will overflow with new wine.* (Proverbs 3:9-10, NASB)

I am a tither.
*"Bring the whole tithe into the storehouse, so that there may be food in My house, and test Me now in this," says the Lord of hosts, "if I will not open for you the windows of heaven and pour out for you a blessing until it overflows."*
(Malachi 3:10, NASB)

I am a great father.
*Train up a child in the way he should go, even when he is old he will not depart from it.* (Proverbs 22:6, NASB)

I am a great mother.
*Train up a child in the way he should go, even when he is old he will not depart from it.* (Proverbs 22:6, NASB)

I am a great son.
*And he said to him, 'Son, you have always been with me, and all that is mine is yours.'* (Luke 15:31, NASB)

I am a great daughter.
*"And he said to him, 'Son, you have always been with me, and all that is mine is yours."* (Luke 15:31, NASB)

I am going to the next level.
*I press on toward the goal for the prize of the upward call of God in Christ Jesus.* (Philippians 3:14, NASB)

I am acquiring property.
*The Lord will command the blessing upon you in your barns and in all that you put your hand to, and He will bless you in the land which the Lord your God gives you.* (Deuteronomy 28:8, NASB)

I am good measure.
*Give, and it will be given to you. They will pour into your lap a good measure—pressed down, shaken together, and running over. For by your standard of measure it will be measured to you in return.* (Luke 6:38, NASB)

I am running over.
*Give, and it will be given to you. They will pour into your lap a good measure—pressed down, shaken together, and running over. For by your standard of measure it will be measured to you in return.* (Luke 6:38, NASB)

I am a son of Zion.
*"I have put My words in your mouth and have covered you with the shadow of My hand, to establish the heavens, to found the earth, and to say to Zion, 'You are My people.'"* (Isaiah 51:16, NASB)

## I Am

I am a worshipper.
*and you shall love the Lord your God with all your heart, and with all your soul, and with all your mind, and with all your strength.* (Mark 12:30, NASB)

I am redeemed.
*Who redeems your life from the pit, Who crowns you with lovingkindness and compassion;* (Psalm 103:4, NASB)

I am thankful.
*Be anxious for nothing, but in everything by prayer and supplication with thanksgiving let your requests be made known to God.* (Philippians 4:6, NASB)

I am victorious.
*The Lord shall cause your enemies who rise up against you to be defeated before you; they will come out against you one way and will flee before you seven ways.* (Deuteronomy 28:7, NASB)

I am favor.
*Blessed shall you be when you come in, and blessed shall you be when you go out.* (Deuteronomy 28:6, NASB)

I am abundance.
*And God is able to make all grace abound to you, so that always having all sufficiency in everything, you may have an abundance for every good deed;* (2 Corinthians 9:8, NASB)

I am happy.
*Then he said to them, "Go, eat of the fat, drink of the sweet, and send portions to him who has nothing prepared; for this day is holy to our Lord. Do not be grieved, for the joy of the Lord is your strength."* (Nehemiah 8:10, NASB)

I am moving forward.
*Brethren, I do not regard myself as having laid hold of it yet; but one thing I do: forgetting what lies behind and reaching forward to what lies ahead,* (Philippians 3:13, NASB)

I am anointed.
*The Spirit of the Lord God is upon me,
Because the Lord has anointed me
To bring good news to the afflicted;
He has sent me to bind up the brokenhearted,
To proclaim liberty to captives
And freedom to prisoners;* (Isaiah 61:1, NASB)

I am a doer of the Word.
*But prove yourselves doers of the word, and not merely hearers who delude themselves.* (James 1:22, NASB)

I am renewed.
*Who satisfies your years with good things, so that your youth is renewed like the eagle.* (Psalm 103:5, NASB)

I am righteous.
*For if by the transgression of the one, death reigned through the one, much more those who receive the abundance of grace and of the gift of righteousness will reign in life through the One, Jesus Christ.* (Romans 5:17, NASB)

I am prophetic.
*Now I wish that you all spoke in tongues, but even more that you would prophesy; and greater is one who prophesies than one who speaks in tongues, unless he interprets, so that the church may receive edifying.* (1 Corinthians 14:5, NASB)

I am breakthrough.
*But about midnight Paul and Silas were praying and singing hymns of praise to God, and the prisoners were listening to them; and suddenly there came a great earthquake, so that the foundations of the prison house were shaken; and immediately ball the doors were opened and everyone's chains were unfastened.* (Acts 16:25-26, NASB)

I am blessed.
*Blessed is the man who trusts in the Lord and whose trust is the Lord.* (Jeremiah 17:7, NASB)

I am a rainmaker.
*Then he prayed again, and the sky poured rain and the earth produced its fruit.* (James 5:18, NASB)

Now that you've read each "I Am" statement with the scripture reference, you can pray the following declaration over your life in its entirety. You can add truth statements from the scripture that speak directly to you. This is a wonderful way to renew your mind with the Word of God.

Ready, Set, Go…

**Declare this out loud:**

I am born again.
I am a new creation.
I am forgiven.
I am called.
I am strong.
I am healed.
I am whole.
I am a healer.

I am a giver.
I am the future.
I am destiny.
I am wonderfully made.
I am rich.
I am wisdom.
I am understanding.
I am revelation knowledge.
I am patience.
I am endurance.
I am a miracle.
I am a wonder.
I am a sign.
I am good news.
I am a treasure.
I am the apple of His eye.
I am peace.
I am obedient.
I am faithful.
I am truthful.
I am perseverant.
I am grace.
I am mercy.
I am justified.
I am provision.
I am prosperity.
I am a tither.
I am a great father.
I am a great mother.
I am a great son.
I am a great daughter.
I am going to the next level.
I am acquiring property.
I am good measure.
I am running over.

# I Am

I am a son of Zion.
I am a worshipper.
I am redeemed.
I am thankful.
I am victorious.
I am favor.
I am abundance.
I am happy.
I am moving forward.
I am anointed.
I am a doer of the Word.
I am renewed.
I am righteous.
I am prophetic.
I am breakthrough.
I am blessed.
I am a rainmaker.

I am the head. I am NOT the tail.
I am above. I am NOT beneath.
I am happy. I am NOT unhappy.
I am rich. I am NOT poor.
I am healed. I am NOT sick.
I am a child. I am NOT an orphan.
I am blessed. I am NOT cursed.
I am promoted. I am NOT demoted.
I am success. I am NOT failure.
I am forgiven. I am NOT condemned.
I am overflow. I am NOT empty.
I am loved. I am NOT alone.
I am strong. I am NOT weak.
I am here. I am NOT forgotten.
I am what God says I am, by the grace of God.

# PART IV

# IT'S TIME TO PRAY

# CHAPTER 8

# INNER CIRCLE PRAYERS

Chapters 8 and 9 are prayers to declare over many aspects of your life. For easy reference, I'll refer to them as "Inner Circle" and "Outer Circle" prayers. Several subjects pertain to both areas and can overlap from time to time, so you should apply them accordingly. These prayers provided are only examples; we will discuss crafting your own later. When combined with your faith, these prayers will help reshape your world. You can then apply the identity statements to these reshaped areas as well. Holy Spirit will partner with you in this as you are being transformed in the image of Jesus.

## Repentance

Heavenly Father, I know You are abundant in mercy and loving kindness. I know if I confess my sin, You are faithful and just and offer forgiveness. You cleanse my body and soul. I come to You today in all humility and covered by the blood of Jesus. I ask for Your forgiveness for the choices I have made and I repent from doing my own will and living from my selfish desires. I want to live daily in Your presence and guidance. I desire to draw near to You, and I apologize for not doing so, allowing the things of life to get in the way of our relationship.

I repent for allowing ungodly thoughts to influence my mind and my actions. I am sorry for treating others less than how You see them and for not loving my neighbor as myself. Forgive me for permitting distractions that hinder my walk with You. I surrender my will, my mind, my body, and my life to You. I want to be a vessel that brings glory to You. I desire to fulfill God's plans and purposes for my life, and I can only do that in complete surrender to You. The finished work of Jesus Christ on the cross purchased my forgiveness and freedom from the ruling entity of sin. As a child of God, I am free from the bondage and chains of sin. The blood of Jesus washes and cleanses me. Today, I commit to living in this truth.

Thank You for loving me. Amen.

One beautiful example of confession, cleansing, and consecration is found in Psalm 51. I recommend reading it in your favorite translation and then again in The Passion Translation. Read it in its entirety so you can see the progression of David bearing his soul before God.

## Psalm 51 Pardon and Purity

(The Passion Translation)

### David's Confession

*God, give me mercy from your fountain of forgiveness!*
*I know your abundant love is enough to wash away my guilt.*
*Because your compassion is so great,*
*take away this shameful guilt of sin.*
*Forgive the full extent of my rebellious ways,*
*and erase this deep stain on my conscience.*
*For I'm so ashamed.*
*I feel such pain and anguish within me.*
*I can't get away from the sting of my sin against you, Lord!*

*Everything I did, I did right in front of you, for you saw it all.*
*Against you, and you above all, have I sinned.*
*Everything you say to me is infallibly true*
*and your judgment conquers me.*
*Lord, I have been a sinner from birth,*
*from the moment my mother conceived me.*
*I know that you delight to set your truth deep in my spirit.*
*So come into the hidden places of my heart*
*and teach me wisdom.*

## David's Cleansing

*Purify my conscience! Make this leper clean again!*
*Wash me in your love until I am pure in heart.*
*Satisfy me in your sweetness, and my song of joy will return.*
*The places within me you have crushed*
*will rejoice in your healing touch.*
*Hide my sins from your face;*
*erase all my guilt by your saving grace.*
*Create a new, clean heart within me.*
*Fill me with pure thoughts and holy desires, ready to please you.*
*May you never reject me!*
*May you never take from me your sacred Spirit!*

## David's Consecration

*Let my passion for life be restored,*
*tasting joy in every breakthrough you bring to me.*
*Hold me close to you with a willing spirit*
*that obeys whatever you say.*
*Then I can show to other guilty ones*
*how loving and merciful you are.*
*They will find their way back home to you,*
*knowing that you will forgive them.*
*O God, my saving God,*

*deliver me fully from every sin,*
*even the sin that brought bloodguilt*
*Then my heart will once again be thrilled to sing*
*the passionate songs of joy and deliverance!*
*Lord God, unlock my heart, unlock my lips,*
*and I will overcome with my joyous praise!*
*For the source of your pleasure is not in my performance*
*or the sacrifices I might offer to you.*
*The fountain of your pleasure is found*
*in the sacrifice of my shattered heart before you.*
*You will not despise my tenderness*
*as I humbly bow down at your feet.*
*Because you favor Zion, do what is good for her.*
*Be the protecting wall around Jerusalem.*
*And when we are fully restored,*
*you will rejoice and take delight*
*in every offering of our lives*
*as we bring our sacrifices of righteousness before you in love!*

## Nighttime

Dear God, thank you for another day of being alive and able to do your will. As I'm about to sleep, I thank you for being with me. I want my mind to be renewed by the Word. Holy Spirit, I welcome you to speak to me so I may receive Your counsel and instruction as I rest. I rebuke every demon that would attempt to attack my sleep or my dreams. The enemy will not be able to disrupt my sleep with fear or anxiety and I will not be restless. May my spirit hear the whispers of Holy Spirit's voice as You lead me tomorrow. I know that You give to me even as I sleep, so I will not worry about the next day. You are my supply, and I'm confident in your provision. Bless me with sound sleep and speak to me in my dreams according to the scripture.

In Jesus Name, Amen.

## Peace

Heavenly Father, I thank you for the gift of peace in my life. Jesus said He gives me the gift of peace, which covers my mind and heart. This peace doesn't come from the things of the world; it only comes from You. I receive Your divine peace today. It is a powerful spiritual weapon which protects me in the circumstances of life. I declare that I have peace in every storm, and I can face any situation. I have peace in my family, my work, my church, my relationships, and every aspect of my life. God's peace rules my thinking and my emotions, and because of this, I am not easily moved by the events surrounding me. I can stand in battle, through the ups and downs of life, and in the raging storms, resting assured that God is with me.

## Joy

I agree with the Word of God saying the joy of the Lord is my strength. I am filled with overflowing joy because Christ is in me with the hope of glory. I am a new wineskin and drink daily from the new wine of heaven. Because of Jesus and the finished works of the cross, I have access to an abundance of joy and peace. You show me the way of life and I have permission from Jesus to be joyful in all seasons. You fill me with bliss in Your presence and the pleasures of living with You forever. As a lover of God, I carry light and joy that burst forth from my heart. I am redeemed, and I can join my voice with heaven's to sing and shout for joy. The sounds of gladness live through me, and they silence my enemy. I receive from the Kingdom of God that is filled with righteousness, peace, and joy in the Holy Spirit.

## Favor

Because I am in Jesus Christ, the favor that is upon Jesus has also been given to me by my Heavenly Father. I am grafted in the Vine, and I am one with Christ. Just as Jesus increased in favor with God and men, I do the same. The favor of God surrounds me as a shield and protects me against enemies on all sides. I believe that I live in the secret place of the Most High and rest in the shadow of the Almighty. He is my refuge and my place of safety; He covers me, and His faithful promises are my protection. I walk in prosperity. People are attracted to me so that I may bless them with what I have. The works of my hands are blessed and established and His favor opens doors of opportunity for me that no man can shut. The Lord is gracious to me so I walk in favor everywhere that I go. I believe that my home, my work, my family, and my ministry are all covered with the presence of God. His goodness and His glory surround me.

## Fear

I live by faith, not by sight. God has not given me a spirit or a mindset of fear. God gives me power, love, and a sound mind, therefore, I rebuke every spirit of fear trying to take root in my heart. I uproot you by the Spirit of God. I am being delivered from fear and worry. I believe that greater is He who lives in me than any power of darkness trying to frighten me. My faith will remain steadfast in times of trouble. Regardless of my circumstances, I declare the safety and protection upon my life because I am a child of the Most High. I rebuke all intimidation from the powers of darkness that are trying to overtake me. I know who I am; I am a son of God and a co-heir with Christ.

## Finances

Today I acknowledge God is my source and my supply. All I have comes from the Lord, the maker of heaven and earth. I declare that I will be grateful for what He provides for me. I want no part of a poverty mindset that devours everything that comes my way. Jesus, may you break off every aspect of poverty that is at work in my life because I want to be a good steward of all You have entrusted to me. The blessing of the Lord makes me rich and adds no sorrow. As I honor You with my possessions and the first fruits of my increase, my life is filled with plenty and overflows with goodness. You have created the law of sowing and reaping. As I plant generously into the Kingdom of God, I will reap provision and abundance in my house and my business. Like Abraham, I am blessed to be a blessing, and I will live a life filled with generosity. The good that I make happen for others, God, will return and make happen for me. I will not covet nor be led by jealousy. The Lord is the One who gives me the power to create wealth. I dedicate all I have to Him and His service. I declare that I am blessed!
    Amen.

## Marriage

Heavenly Father, I am thankful for my marriage. You have provided this covenant union that reflects our covenant relationship with You. I am grateful for my spouse. Help me to learn how to love better and be the spouse you have intended me to be. Help us to walk in a bond of unity and peace and protect us from the things that will divide us. We chose to forgive one another as You have forgiven us, so help us to grow in humility and to work through our differences in a way that honors You and one another. Bring strength to every weak area of our marriage. May we grow in communion with you each day. May we live according to the fruit of the Spirit and love each other by your Word. Guide us daily that we may not fall into temptation; cover and protect us when we are apart from one another. Teach us to love one another unconditionally and help us recognize our marriage as holy and with a divine purpose. Reveal to us the beauty and joy of our relationship each day and may Your gift of peace reign in our home. I declare that my marriage is blessed.

## Children

My children are a love-gift from the Lord, a generous reward from my Heavenly Father. I believe they will grow in wisdom and stature and increase in favor with God and with people. I bless my children. I pray they will have a deeply personal relationship with Jesus and will live in obedience to the things of God. I decree all generational curses are broken from their lives, so they will walk in freedom and blessing. I decree my children will be saved from sin and not out of sin. Gracious Father, I ask you in the name of Jesus that no harm, no danger, and no disabling accident happen to my children when they are away from me. May You cover and protect them each day and assign Your angels to guard them in all their ways. I declare the promises of the Lord will be fulfilled in their lives. I bless my children to walk in the fullness of God, and I declare they will be revivalists and carriers of God's glory.

Amen.

## Health

The scripture teaches that healing is the children's bread, and therefore as a child of God, I receive total health in my body. Jesus paid the price for my healing; He purchased it over 2,000 years ago by the finished works of the cross. His body was broken, and His blood was shed so that I could live in wholeness here on earth and in eternity with Him. The Lord forgives all my sins and heals all my diseases. He redeems my life. The sun of righteousness rises over me with healing in its wings. As my days are, so will my strength be. Jesus has sent forth His word to heal me and has rescued me from death, hell, and the grave. The Lord has not given me a spirit of fear, but of power, love, and a sound mind. I am strong in the Lord and the power of His might. I walk in divine health and healing today. Every organ in my body is rejuvenated and receives the healing power of Jesus. Every cell in my bloodstream radiates with healing and life. Sickness and disease cannot live in my body. All forms of cancer, disease, and illness must be eliminated from my body as total healing pours over me. I received complete physical, mental, and emotional health in the name of Jesus Christ.

Amen.

## Wisdom and Revelation

Heavenly Father, I thank You for hearing me every time I call on Your name. I pray in the name of Jesus that You would give me a spirit of wisdom and revelation. I want to know You more intimately. You promised I can ask for wisdom and it will be granted to me; You will not reject me. I humble myself and ask for a teachable spirit and for the revelation of my inheritance on the next stage of my journey with You. As I mediate on the Word and remain in Your presence, please grant me inspiration and insight. Establish my inheritance as I am a co-heir with Christ. I want to experience spiritual growth and I seek the gifts of knowledge and wisdom. Raise me to a higher level in the Spirit so my heart would be increased with Your confidence. Open the eyes of my heart so I can see You and Your purposes. I ask that You fill me with spiritual wisdom and insight that I may grow in the knowledge God. Holy Spirit lead me into all truth.

In Jesus name, Amen.

## The Finished Work of the Cross

Today I am grateful, and I remind myself of the truth that has set me free. Through the blood of Jesus Christ, I am redeemed out of the hand of the devil. Jesus used His servant body to carry my sins to the cross for my salvation. He suffered for my sake. Jesus was pierced for my transgressions; He was crushed for my iniquity. He endured the punishment that made me completely whole and with the stripes that wounded Him, I am healed. Through the blood of Jesus all my sins are forgiven. The blood of Jesus Christ cleanses me continually from all sin. Because of Jesus and the finished work of the cross, I am justified, made righteous, just as if I had never sinned. Because of Jesus and the finished work of the cross, I am sanctified, made holy, and set apart to God. My body is a temple for the Holy Spirit. I am redeemed and cleansed. I have the promise of healing spiritually, emotionally, and physically from all sickness and disease. Satan has no place in me and no power over me. Through the power of Jesus Christ, I renounce Satan, loose myself from the powers of darkness and command all demonic entities to leave me. The finished work of Christ on the cross is the power of God to bring me everlasting life. It is divine, holy, perfect and complete. The finished work of Christ on the cross brings me forgiveness and victory. I receive a new nature and live under a New Covenant. Every argument brought against me is canceled and I live in blessing and no longer under a curse.

Thank You, Jesus, for all You have done for me.

## Communion

*For I received from the Lord what I also delivered to you, that the Lord Jesus on the night when he was betrayed took bread, and when he had given thanks, he broke it, and said, "This is my body, which is for you. Do this in remembrance of me." In the same way also he took the cup, after supper, saying, "This cup is the new covenant in my blood. Do this, as often as you drink it, in remembrance of me." For as often as you eat this bread and drink the cup, you proclaim the Lord's death until he comes.* (1 Corinthians 11:23-26, ESV)

*To partake, first, hold the bread in your hand and say:*

Thank You, Father, for the gift of Your Son. By the stripes that fell on His back, my body is healed from the crown of my head to the very soles of my feet. Every cell, every organ, every function of my body is healed, restored, and renewed. I receive Your divine supply in every aspect of my life. In Jesus' name, I believe and I receive.

[Eat the bread]

*Next, take the cup in your hand and say:*

Lord Jesus, thank You for Your precious blood. Your shed blood has removed every sin from my life. Through Your blood, I am forgiven of all my sins—past, present, and future—and made completely righteous. Today, I celebrate and partake of the inheritance of the righteous, which is preservation, healing, wholeness, and provision. Thank You, Lord, for loving me. Amen.

[Drink the cup]

## Recovery

Heavenly Father, I come to you today as your child. Regardless of my current circumstance, I know who I am in Christ. I have a rightful inheritance because I am a co-heir with Christ. Because of Jesus, I know I am allowed to come boldly before the Throne of Grace. I believe that You will give me what I ask according to Your will.

You have always made a way for me. You make rivers in the desert and roads in the wilderness. You can restore all that has been lost or stolen in my life, including lost years. You can open doors of opportunity that I have missed along the way. Please grant me a season of recovery. I declare that I will recover all that has been lost and stolen by the enemy in my life. Every work of darkness and every evil that has ravished my life has now come to an end. I rebuke the spirit of intimidation that has tried to overtake me. I declare to every spiritual enemy that I will get everything back that has been lost or stolen from my family and me. I will not stop repossessing everything until it's all accomplished.

I am stepping into a season of recovery and repayment, without fail. Restoration is mine because of the grace of Jesus Christ. My entire family will change for the good. My job is becoming better each day and my income is increasing as I walk in blessing. I am a faithful steward of all that has been given to me by the Lord.

I declare that I am strong in the Lord, in the power of His might. I am a son of the King of Glory, and therefore I walk in the recovery of all things taken from me. By the Spirit of God, I recover finances, possessions, opportunities, children, parents, friendships. I have renewed health, and where my body has been attacked with sickness and disease, I receive a full recovery. I break every curse and demonic assignment against the promises of God in my life. I now walk in the blessing of restoration and recovery.

Thank You, Jesus!

## When you don't know what to pray, offer supplication to the Lord

Father, I come to You in the precious name of Jesus and praise You for these circumstances. I thank You for being with me and for me. I know that You have a plan and a purpose for me and You have a desire to help me right now. Please show me Your ways that I may walk in Your truth. Teach me the path to walk and show me Your divine will. My desire is to be conformed into the image of Jesus, especially in this situation. I want to cooperate with Your will and not resist You in any way. I will joyously praise You even when I'm not sure what else to do and will renew my mind with the Word. May my spirit be open to hear Your thoughts because I want to obey your plan. I surrender my will. I don't lean on my own understanding, and I do trust You with all of My heart. Lead me and guide me.

Thank You and Amen.

# CHAPTER 9

# OUTER CIRCLE PRAYERS

The previous chapter addresses what I refer to as the "Inner Circle" areas of life. This chapter will expand that to cover your "Outer Circle" prayer needs. Several subjects pertain to both areas and can overlap from time to time, so you should apply them accordingly. These prayers provided are only examples. As stated earlier, when combined with your faith, these prayers will help reshape your world.

## Friends

Lord Jesus, I thank you that you value friendship. Teach me to be friendly to others first and to love them the way You have loved me. As I build relationships with others, allow them to see Christ in me in all aspects of my life. Because Godly friendships are important, bring friendships to me that will strengthen my life and will enable me to be the same to them. Bless me with "iron sharpens iron" relationships. Help me to be vulnerable and authentic in my conversations with friends I can genuinely trust. As I become more aware that I am a friend of God, help me to be a true friend of others, shining through me in my relationships. Grant me deep connections with my friends, and may You always be the center of it all. Help me to walk in kindness, gentleness, love, and trustworthiness in these relationships.

In Jesus name, Amen.

## Reconciliation

Dear Jesus, help me to obey the commands You have given, to love God first and to love my neighbor as myself. I ask Your forgiveness for where I've fallen short in doing this. Because You have given all Christ followers the ministry and message of reconciliation, I receive the grace to be active in it. I will be one who connects people back to You. I want to also be a peacemaker who reconciles relationships. I am an ambassador of the Kingdom of God where every nation, tribe, language, and people are celebrated as equal.

I understand that my struggle is not against flesh and blood, but against spiritual rulers, authorities, demonic powers of this present darkness, and forces of evil. They keep racism alive in systems, institutions, and spreading the lie that some members of humanity are inferior and others superior. I choose to put on the whole armor of God, so I am able to stand against the schemes of the devil.

Help me to walk in love and treat everyone I come in contact with as someone that You love dearly. Examine my heart Lord to identify any prejudice that I am unaware. Give me a heart of compassion for people, especially for those who are different than me. Create in me a new mind and heart that will rid myself of prejudice and racial stereotypes. Help me to never contribute to oppression. Help me to walk in humility and not entitlement. Use me as a vessel of racial reconciliation that heals the wounds of others and brings people together. May the love of Christ flow through me so others experience the life changing power of that love. Enable me to see brothers and sisters in the faces of those divided by culture, ethnicity and skin color.

In Your name, Amen.

## Education

Father, I am grateful You provide everything I need for gaining wisdom and instruction according to Your Word. I ask that you bless my education. Guide me as I choose classes and a career path that would lead me to success and, most importantly, help fulfill Your will in my life. Bless my mind to remember the things I've studied so I may grow in knowledge. Help me gain favor so I may be salt and light to my classmates; may I build solid friendships based upon righteousness. I declare that God's glory and protection reign in my school. I also pray for financial provision to cover any education costs.
In Jesus name, Amen.

## For Child's Education

Heavenly Father, I thank You for my child(ren). I do know children are a gift from you. I am grateful to have this responsibility and Your trust to raise them in a God-fearing manner. I bless them today as they learn and pray they may grow in knowledge and favor. I bless their brains to grasp new concepts and to learn new skills. May their minds remember all the things that they've studied. I speak a blessing over their teachers and their classmates so they can build solid friendships based upon righteousness and kindness. May they be protected from bullying and not fall into temptation from negative peer pressure. I pray my child(ren) respond in compassion, respect, and act in Christlike behavior. May they be salt and light in their school. Please cover and protect them each day and assign Your angels to guard them in all their ways. I ask you in the name of Jesus that no harm, no danger, and no disabling accident happen to my children when they are away from me.
Amen.

## Influences

Lord, I surrender every aspect of my life to You. Teach me Your ways and speak to my heart because You invite me to abide in You and You in me. Instruct me in all my decisions and guide my ideas.

I submit my relationships to You. Show me any relationship that isn't holy or honoring and give me the grace to know how to navigate it. Keep me from trouble and harm. Send brothers and sisters in Christ to help disciple me and to help me be an example to others. If there's a relationship in need of change, give me the grace to fix it in a manner that pleases you.

In Jesus name, Amen.

## Work

Heavenly Father, I am grateful for the opportunity to work and earn wages. Thank You for my job. I ask You to bless my employer to be successful, especially because I am there and represent Your Kingdom. I speak a blessing over everything my hand touches and areas I influence in my workplace. Help me extend Your plans and purposes each day. May I do everything in my job for the glory of God according to Your word.

Help me advance in my career and remain humble in my success. As I enter the workplace, I want to carry Your tangible presence with me. Anoint my ideas and efforts, and may they be a blessing to my career path and those I serve. I declare the favor of God surrounds me as a shield and goes before me each day. Thank you for contracts, sales, commissions, projects, ideas, inventions, and anything else that would bless me in my endeavors. May I be salt and light in this establishment. Help me to make ethical decisions, deals, and relationships so I can bring glory to You at my workplace.

In Jesus name, Amen.

## Hope is Not Deferred

Today I choose to believe the promises of God over my life and environment and bask in His faithfulness. Today I receive clarity from Holy Spirit in every unclear area of my life. I have hope for the present and for the future. My hope is not deferred in my promise. There are generational blessings upon the lives of God's people. I am a child of God, and I am grafted in the Vine. Indeed, the Lord watches over the whole earth to strengthen those whose hearts are fully committed to Him. He sees me because my heart is completely His. I come into agreement with His thoughts and desires in my life, and therefore, I am flooded with hope. My entire family will share in the blessings of the Lord for generations to come and His promises will become our testimonies. My hope is at the forefront of God's purpose for my life.

Amen.

## Spiritual Battles

Heavenly Father, Your Word tells me not to fear. Your Word tells me that as your child, the battle is not mine, but Yours. I am not alone—Your presence surrounds me. I declare that I am a mighty prayer warrior, and I partner with God's divine purpose for my life. When I pray, God releases spiritual assistance and the power of grace in my circumstances. I thank You for giving Your angels charge over me and for Your divine aid and protection. I ask You to release angels over situations in my life and help me battle against spirits of darkness.

Through the power of Jesus Christ, I renounce Satan, loose myself from the powers of darkness and command all demonic entities to leave me. The finished work of Christ on the cross is the power of God to bring me everlasting life. It is divine, holy, perfect and complete. The finished work of

Christ on the cross brings me and victory. Every argument brought against me is canceled and I live in blessing, no longer under a curse. Because God is my refuge and my dwelling place, evil cannot get close enough to harm me. Even if I stumble, His angels will keep me from falling. Because I love and delight in the Lord, He will protect me. He answers my cry for help every time I pray, so I can anticipate His enveloping presence, even in times of trouble. I thank You for every spiritual blessing provided in my life. God is my glorious hero and He will fight my battles.

## Renounce Demonic Influence

Holy Spirit, please show me if I have any active demonic oppression or open doors to the demonic in my life. (listen to what Holy Spirit identifies)

I repent for giving place to demons in my life. (list them)

I forgive myself for the pain and limitations I have allowed demons to inflict on me.

In the name of Jesus, I renounce and break all agreements with demons and strongholds, and break every contract with evil. I take authority over them now and command all strongholds and all associated demons to leave me now in the name of Jesus. I have this authority as a believer based on the finished work of Jesus Christ on the cross.

Heavenly Father, I thank You for giving Your angels charge over me. I thank You for divine assistance and protection. I ask you to release Your angels over situations in my life and help me battle against spirits of darkness. I thank You for every spiritual blessing provided in my life.

## Spiritual Warfare

Father, in the name of Jesus, I thank You for the promises You have over my life. I thank You for the prophetic words and purposes you have spoken over me, and I use them as weapons of war against demonic forces coming against me. I break the evil powers that want to manifest, manipulate, resist, limit, set back, and bring disappointment to me. I cancel all demonic assignments over my life. I superimpose God's perfect will over the fear of the unknown, over the walls of opposition and resistance, and over demonic predictions and projections. I declare that the blood of Jesus protects me. Through the power of the blood of Jesus, I overrule, nullify, and revoke the plans of darkness. I silence the accuser and strike down the intimidation of fear. Thank You, Lord, for victory! Amen.

# PART V

# MAKE IT PERSONAL

# CHAPTER 10

# CRAFTING PRAYERS

Craft your own prayers and decrees. The process is simple and provides an opportunity for you to partner with the Holy Spirit. When we write our own prayer, any aspect of life can be used for our spiritual growth because God is for us in every situation. According to Romans 8, there's nothing that can separate us from God's love in Christ Jesus. Neither death nor life, angels nor demons, fears of today or worries of tomorrow, nor anything else in the world. It doesn't matter what we are facing; God has made us more than conquerors. We can pray boldly because heaven is listening, and God wants to partner with us.

I encourage you to go through areas of your life and inquire of the Lord, "What should I be praying for in this situation?" Ask Him to reveal the intentions of His heart over your life. Search the scriptures for His heart pertaining to what you are going through. As the Father, what prayer would help release His power and presence in your life? Then, write and pray. Continue doing this until your spirit bears witness with the Holy Spirit, then adjust accordingly. You will find yourself in tune with the heart of God, and your prayers and decrees will become something you enjoy. You will see results as heaven invades earth over your life.

*And this is the confidence (the assurance, the privilege of boldness) which we have in Him: [we are sure] that if we ask anything (make any request) according to His will (in agreement with His own plan), He listens to and hears us.*

*And if (since) we [positively] know that He listens to us in whatever we ask, we also know [with settled and absolute knowledge] that we have [granted us as our present possessions] the requests made of Him.* (1 John 5:14-15, AMP)

We can be confident God hears us and grants our requests according to His plan and purposes. He listens to us and desires we understand His heart to know what to pray and declare. This partnership is powerful and beautiful invitation.

Things to consider when crafting a decree for your life:

1. What's the situation?
2. Ask God to reveal the intentions of His heart over the matter.
3. What does the Bible say concerning it? Verses?
4. What is your desired outcome?
5. What decree can you make according to the scripture?
6. Craft a prayer.
7. Ask the Lord if it aligns with His will.
8. Submit the prayer to the Lord as ask Him if anything needs adjusted or clarified.
9. Pray. Pray. Pray.
10. Decree. Decree. Decree.

11. Proclaim with confidence what God has revealed until the resolution comes.

## Craft your prayer

What is the situation?

_____

_____

_____

Ask God to reveal the intentions of His heart over the matter.

_____

_____

_____

What does the Bible say concerning it? Verses?

_____

_____

_____

What is your desired outcome?

_____

_____

_____

What decree can you make according to the scripture?

_____

_____

_____

Craft a prayer.

_____

_____

_____

_____

_____

_____

_____

_____

_____

_____

Ask the Lord if it aligns with His will.

_____

_____

_____

Submit the prayer to the Lord as ask Him if anything needs adjusted or clarified.

___

___

___

Pray. Pray. Pray.

Decree. Decree. Decree.

## Craft your prayer

What is the situation?

___

___

___

Ask God to reveal the intentions of His heart over the matter.

___

___

___

What does the Bible say concerning it? Verses?

___

___

___

# Voice-Activated

What is your desired outcome?

_____

_____

_____

What decree can you make according to the scripture?

_____

_____

_____

Craft a prayer.

_____

_____

_____

_____

_____

_____

_____

Ask the Lord if it aligns with His will.

_____

_____

_____

Submit the prayer to the Lord as ask Him if anything needs adjusted or clarified.

_____
_____
_____

Pray. Pray. Pray.

Decree. Decree. Decree.

## Craft your prayer

What is the situation?

_____
_____
_____

Ask God to reveal the intentions of His heart over the matter.

_____
_____
_____

What does the Bible say concerning it? Verses?

_____
_____
_____

What is your desired outcome?

_____
_____
_____

What decree can you make according to the scripture?

_____
_____
_____

Craft a prayer.

_____
_____
_____
_____
_____
_____
_____

Ask the Lord if it aligns with His will.

_____
_____
_____

Submit the prayer to the Lord as ask Him if anything needs adjusted or clarified.

___

Pray. Pray. Pray.

Decree. Decree. Decree.

## Craft your prayer

What is the situation?

___

Ask God to reveal the intentions of His heart over the matter.

___

What does the Bible say concerning it? Verses?

___

What is your desired outcome?

_____

_____

_____

What decree can you make according to the scripture?

_____

_____

_____

Craft a prayer.

_____

_____

_____

_____

_____

_____

_____

Ask the Lord if it aligns with His will.

_____

_____

_____

## Crafting Prayers

Submit the prayer to the Lord as ask Him if anything needs adjusted or clarified.

_____

_____

_____

Pray. Pray. Pray.

Decree. Decree. Decree.

# CHAPTER 11

# CONCLUSION: THE CHALLENGE

Remember earlier when I mentioned the 30 day, 60 day, and 180 day challenges? I hope you are ready to join in the fun. It's time to accept a spiritual challenge.

Consider how 30 days of praying for a specific topic could impact you, or what the outcome could be if you declared God's perspective in a few areas of your life for 60 days.

Could your life be revolutionized if you had a dedicated approach to prayer for 180 days?

I believe the answer is an emphatic YES.

I've created a few examples below so you can customize them to whatever your current circumstances are. I recommend you add praying in tongues to this daily challenge.

I also highly recommend participating in Holy Communion on a regular basis, at least a few times per week. You can do this personally and/or with your immediate family. Be sure to use the Communion prayer in Chapter 8.

## 30 Day Challenge

Let's consider the topics of Sleep and Rest. These are vital to the functions of your body and soul.

Before bedtime, read some of the scriptures listed under **Sleep** in Chapter 6.

Declare the **Nighttime** prayer from Chapter 8.

In the morning read the **Peace** prayer from Chapter 8.

Of course, you need to do this out loud. Remember, you and your surroundings are voice-activated. Pray in tongues as well.

Do this for 30 days, then evaluate your sleep quality and the level of peace you are living under. Take time along the way to journal your experience.

## 60 Day Challenge

Let's consider the importance of our identity in Christ. This influences every area of our lives and it takes time to renew our minds to these powerful truths. Most of the time, our life circumstances and the world's system contradict areas of God's design.

Read the **I Am Decrees** in Chapter 7. Which items stand out the most? When you find statements you know need to be reinforced in your life, write them down.

Study them with their supporting scriptures referred to in Chapter 7.

Take at least 15-20 minutes, or whatever time you need, to decree the statements and their scripture references. Don't rush through them as if you are just reading a list. These are areas that make a deep impact on your spirit and your soul, so let them settle in. Read the scripture to yourself, then read it again out loud. Declare the **I Am Decrees** with conviction and belief. Pray in tongues as well.

Doing this for 60 days will allow you to memorize not only the statement, but many of the scriptures as well. This becomes a powerful weapon against the enemy and creates unconscious confidence to live out these truths.

Listen to Holy Spirit in this season because He reveals the heart of the Father. Take time along the way to journal your experience.

## 180 Day Challenge

After completing either a 30 day or 60 day challenge, it's time to take a voyage. The next six months of your life can be revolutionized. It may not be easy, but if you stay the course you will discover so much that God has for you.

I recommend doing this in three, 60 day sections. You can follow the two examples listed above to get started. Ask Holy Spirit which areas to focus on. He will guide and teach you along the way.

Here's an example:

60 days of *inner circle* decrees. Choose 2-3 areas specific to your daily life. Take time along the way to journal your experience.

Then, 60 days of *outer circle* decrees. Choose 2-3 areas that are part of your surroundings. Make sure to include some of the spiritual warfare aspects because you want to break through any resistance of spiritual darkness. Take time along the way to journal your experience.

Now it's time for the last 60 day section, *bold* decrees. Review your journal to see the progress you've made. Are there any areas you still struggle with? If so, you can keep them on the list. Family dynamics can take longer to see change, so marriage dilemmas or struggles with children may stay on your list for a while. Don't quit! There are extra complexities to home matters because of personalities, spiritual lives, and any access given to demonic forces. As you continue to pray the intentions of God's heart over these areas, you will see impact.

Revisit **ungodly beliefs** in Chapter 5. Ask Holy Spirit if you still have any ungodly beliefs, especially concerning the last 120 days of this voyage. Once identified, take the time to repent, renounce, and hear from the Lord a new Godly belief you can replace it with. Find supporting scripture that will help renew your mind.

## Conclusion: The Challenge

In the final 60 days of this challenge, it's time to pray *bold* prayers. Whether they are about finances, favor, employment etc., this is the time to pray big. God is able and willing to release more to us than we can ask for or imagine. Recognize your spiritual authority over the powers of darkness and use it. Allow your faith to increase as you discover new ways to pray and find decrees in the scripture you can apply to your life.

When you craft your own prayers, notice how the atmosphere changes around you and how God's presence becomes more tangible. This doesn't mean life becomes perfect or storms and trials aren't active, but it does mean you have an opportunity to travel differently through them all. Your partnership with Heaven will become a greater reality and you will be equipped like never before.

Again, take time along the way to journal your experience and remember to pray in tongues as well. Proclaim with confidence what God has revealed until the resolution comes.

Thank you for taking the time to read this book. You have the opportunity to reshape your life by making daily declarations, placing you on a pathway to defining your future. You have learned the power of words and how to use them properly. There is a new world waiting for your arrival. I pray you become more voice-activated than ever before.

# WORKS CITED

*New American Standard Bible: 1995 update.* (1995). (John 6:63). La Habra, CA: The Lockman Foundation.

*New American Standard Bible: 1995 update.* (1995). (Proverbs 18:21). La Habra, CA: The Lockman Foundation.

*New American Standard Bible: 1995 update.* (1995). (Ephesians 4:29-32). La Habra, CA: The Lockman Foundation.

*New American Standard Bible: 1995 update.* (1995). (John 1:1-2). La Habra, CA: The Lockman Foundation.

*New American Standard Bible: 1995 update.* (1995). (John 1:14). La Habra, CA: The Lockman Foundation.

*New American Standard Bible: 1995 update.* (1995). (Psalm 55:21). La Habra, CA: The Lockman Foundation.

*The Holy Bible: New International Version.* (1984). (Proverbs 12:18). Grand Rapids, MI: Zondervan.

*New American Standard Bible: 1995 update.* (1995). (Ephesians 6:17). La Habra, CA: The Lockman Foundation.

*New American Standard Bible: 1995 update.* (1995). (Revelation 12:11). La Habra, CA: The Lockman Foundation.

*New American Standard Bible: 1995 update.* (1995). (Philippians 4:4). La Habra, CA: The Lockman Foundation.

*The New King James Version.* (1982). (Isaiah 55:10-11, NKJV) Nashville: Thomas Nelson.

*New American Standard Bible: 1995 update.* (1995). (Proverbs 12:14). La Habra, CA: The Lockman Foundation.

*New American Standard Bible: 1995 update.* (1995). (Psalm 103:19-21). La Habra, CA: The Lockman Foundation.

*The Amplified Bible.* (1987). (Hebrews 1:14). La Habra, CA: The Lockman Foundation.

*The Amplified Bible.* (1987). (Hebrews 1:14). La Habra, CA: The Lockman Foundation.

*The Amplified Bible.* (1987). (Psalm 39:7). La Habra, CA: The Lockman Foundation.

*The Holy Bible: English Standard Version.* (2016). (Gen 1:2). Wheaton, IL: Crossway Bibles.

Simmons, B. (Trans.). (2017). *The Passion Translation: New Testament* (Ephesians 1:3). BroadStreet Publishing.

*The Holy Bible: English Standard Version.* (2016). (Romans 4:16-21). Wheaton, IL: Crossway Bibles.

*The Amplified Bible.* (1987). (1 Corinthians 14:15). La Habra, CA: The Lockman Foundation.

# Works Cited

*New American Standard Bible: 1995 update.* (1995). (John 4:10). La Habra, CA: The Lockman Foundation.

*New American Standard Bible: 1995 update.* (1995). (John 4:13-14). La Habra, CA: The Lockman Foundation.

*New American Standard Bible: 1995 update.* (1995). (John 7:37-39). La Habra, CA: The Lockman Foundation.

*New American Standard Bible: 1995 update.* (1995). (1 Corinthians 12:13). La Habra, CA: The Lockman Foundation.

*New American Standard Bible: 1995 update.* (1995). (1 Corinthians 14:2). La Habra, CA: The Lockman Foundation.

*New American Standard Bible: 1995 update.* (1995). (Romans 8:26-27). La Habra, CA: The Lockman Foundation.

*New American Standard Bible: 1995 update.* (1995). (Jude 20). La Habra, CA: The Lockman Foundation.

*Merriam-Webster's Collegiate® Dictionary, Eleventh Edition*, Edition by Merriam-Webster published by Merriam-Webster, Inc. (**2003**) the *Merriam-Webster.com Dictionary*

*The New King James Version.* (1982). (Ps 91:1–4). Nashville: Thomas Nelson.

*New American Standard Bible: 1995 update.* (1995). (Job 22:27-28). La Habra, CA: The Lockman Foundation.

*The Holy Bible: English Standard Version.* (2016). (2 Kings 2:19-22). Wheaton, IL: Crossway Bibles.

*The Holy Bible: English Standard Version.* (2016). (Joshua 6:26). Wheaton, IL: Crossway Bibles.

*The Holy Bible: English Standard Version.* (2016). (1 Kings 16:33-34). Wheaton, IL: Crossway Bibles.

Tyndale House Publishers. (2015). *Holy Bible: New Living Translation* (Ephesians 1:3). Carol Stream, IL: Tyndale House Publishers.

The Hidden Messages in Water, Masaru Emoto (2001) English translation (2004) by Beyond Words Publishing, translated by David A. Thayne

Tyndale House Publishers. (2015). *Holy Bible: New Living Translation* (1 Pe 1:6–7). Carol Stream, IL: Tyndale House Publishers.

*The Holy Bible: English Standard Version.* (2016). (Pr 12:14). Wheaton, IL: Crossway Bibles.

Tyndale House Publishers. (2015). *Holy Bible: New Living Translation* (2 Co 11:25–27). Carol Stream, IL: Tyndale House Publishers.

Tyndale House Publishers. (2015). *Holy Bible: New Living Translation* (Mt 8:23–26). Carol Stream, IL: Tyndale House Publishers.

*The Holy Bible: English Standard Version.* (2016). (Mk 4:39). Wheaton, IL: Crossway Bibles.

# Works Cited

Tyndale House Publishers. (2015). *Holy Bible: New Living Translation* (Eph 1:3). Carol Stream, IL: Tyndale House Publishers.

*The Amplified Bible.* (1987). (Romans 6:4-5). La Habra, CA: The Lockman Foundation.

*The Amplified Bible.* (1987). (Romans 8:17). La Habra, CA: The Lockman Foundation.

*The Amplified Bible.* (1987). (Ephesians 2:6). La Habra, CA: The Lockman Foundation.

*New American Standard Bible: 1995 update.* (1995). (John 3:3). La Habra, CA: The Lockman Foundation.

*New American Standard Bible: 1995 update.* (1995). (2 Corinthians 5:17). La Habra, CA: The Lockman Foundation.

*New American Standard Bible: 1995 update.* (1995). (Psalm 103:3). La Habra, CA: The Lockman Foundation.

*New American Standard Bible: 1995 update.* (1995). (Deuteronomy 28:10). La Habra, CA: The Lockman Foundation.

*New American Standard Bible: 1995 update.* (1995). (Ephesians 6:10). La Habra, CA: The Lockman Foundation.

*New American Standard Bible: 1995 update.* (1995). (1 Peter 2:24). La Habra, CA: The Lockman Foundation.

*New American Standard Bible: 1995 update.* (1995). (1 Thessalonians 5:23). La Habra, CA: The Lockman Foundation.

*New American Standard Bible: 1995 update.* (1995). (Matthew 10:8). La Habra, CA: The Lockman Foundation.

*New American Standard Bible: 1995 update.* (1995). (Luke 6:38). La Habra, CA: The Lockman Foundation.

*New American Standard Bible: 1995 update.* (1995). (John 15:16). La Habra, CA: The Lockman Foundation.

*New American Standard Bible: 1995 update.* (1995). (Jeremiah 1:5). La Habra, CA: The Lockman Foundation.

*New American Standard Bible: 1995 update.* (1995). (Psalm 139:14). La Habra, CA: The Lockman Foundation.

*New American Standard Bible: 1995 update.* (1995). (2 Corinthians 8:9). La Habra, CA: The Lockman Foundation.

*New American Standard Bible: 1995 update.* (1995). (I Corinthians 1:30). La Habra, CA: The Lockman Foundation.

*New American Standard Bible: 1995 update.* (1995). (1 John 4:6). La Habra, CA: The Lockman Foundation.

*New American Standard Bible: 1995 update.* (1995). (Ephesians 1:17). La Habra, CA: The Lockman Foundation.

*New American Standard Bible: 1995 update.* (1995). (Colossians 1:11-12). La Habra, CA: The Lockman Foundation.

# Works Cited

*New American Standard Bible: 1995 update.* (1995). (Matthew 10:8). La Habra, CA: The Lockman Foundation.

*New American Standard Bible: 1995 update.* (1995). (Acts 4:30). La Habra, CA: The Lockman Foundation.

*New American Standard Bible: 1995 update.* (1995). (Isaiah 52:7). La Habra, CA: The Lockman Foundation.

*New American Standard Bible: 1995 update.* (1995). (Psalm 135:4). La Habra, CA: The Lockman Foundation.

*New American Standard Bible: 1995 update.* (1995). (Zechariah 2:8). La Habra, CA: The Lockman Foundation.

*New American Standard Bible: 1995 update.* (1995). (2 Thessalonians 3:16). La Habra, CA: The Lockman Foundation.

*New American Standard Bible: 1995 update.* (1995). (Deuteronomy 28:2). La Habra, CA: The Lockman Foundation.

*New American Standard Bible: 1995 update.* (1995). (Luke 16:10). La Habra, CA: The Lockman Foundation.

*New American Standard Bible: 1995 update.* (1995). (2 Timothy 2:15). La Habra, CA: The Lockman Foundation.

*New American Standard Bible: 1995 update.* (1995). (Philippians 3:12). La Habra, CA: The Lockman Foundation.

*New American Standard Bible: 1995 update.* (1995). (2 Corinthians 9:8). La Habra, CA: The Lockman Foundation.

*New American Standard Bible: 1995 update.* (1995). (Luke 6:36). La Habra, CA: The Lockman Foundation.

*New American Standard Bible: 1995 update.* (1995). (Romans 5:18). La Habra, CA: The Lockman Foundation.

*New American Standard Bible: 1995 update.* (1995). (Psalm 132:15). La Habra, CA: The Lockman Foundation.

*New American Standard Bible: 1995 update.* (1995). (Proverbs 3:9-10). La Habra, CA: The Lockman Foundation.

*New American Standard Bible: 1995 update.* (1995). (Malachi 3:10). La Habra, CA: The Lockman Foundation.

*New American Standard Bible: 1995 update.* (1995). (Proverbs 22:6). La Habra, CA: The Lockman Foundation.

*New American Standard Bible: 1995 update.* (1995). (Luke 15:31). La Habra, CA: The Lockman Foundation.

*New American Standard Bible: 1995 update.* (1995). (Philippians 3:14 La Habra, CA: The Lockman Foundation.

*New American Standard Bible: 1995 update.* (1995). (Deuteronomy 28:8). La Habra, CA: The Lockman Foundation.

*New American Standard Bible: 1995 update.* (1995). (Luke 6:38). La Habra, CA: The Lockman Foundation.

*New American Standard Bible: 1995 update.* (1995). (Isaiah 51:16). La Habra, CA: The Lockman Foundation.

## Works Cited

*New American Standard Bible: 1995 update.* (1995). (Mark 12:30). La Habra, CA: The Lockman Foundation.

*New American Standard Bible: 1995 update.* (1995). (Philippians 4:6). La Habra, CA: The Lockman Foundation.

*New American Standard Bible: 1995 update.* (1995). (Deuteronomy 28:7). La Habra, CA: The Lockman Foundation.

*New American Standard Bible: 1995 update.* (1995). (Deuteronomy 28:6). La Habra, CA: The Lockman Foundation.

*New American Standard Bible: 1995 update.* (1995). (2 Corinthians 9:8). La Habra, CA: The Lockman Foundation.

*New American Standard Bible: 1995 update.* (1995). (Nehemiah 8:10). La Habra, CA: The Lockman Foundation.

*New American Standard Bible: 1995 update.* (1995). (Philippians 3:13). La Habra, CA: The Lockman Foundation.

*New American Standard Bible: 1995 update.* (1995). (Isaiah 61:1). La Habra, CA: The Lockman Foundation.

*New American Standard Bible: 1995 update.* (1995). (James 1:22). La Habra, CA: The Lockman Foundation.

*New American Standard Bible: 1995 update.* (1995). (Psalm 103:5). La Habra, CA: The Lockman Foundation.

*New American Standard Bible: 1995 update.* (1995). (Romans 5:17). La Habra, CA: The Lockman Foundation.

*New American Standard Bible: 1995 update.* (1995). (1 Corinthians 14:5). La Habra, CA: The Lockman Foundation.

*New American Standard Bible: 1995 update.* (1995). (Acts 16:25-26). La Habra, CA: The Lockman Foundation.

*New American Standard Bible: 1995 update.* (1995). (James 5:18). La Habra, CA: The Lockman Foundation.

*New American Standard Bible: 1995 update.* (1995). (Job 33:15-16). La Habra, CA: The Lockman Foundation.

Simmons, B. (Trans.). (2017). *The Passion Translation: New Testament* (Psalm 16:7 TPT). BroadStreet Publishing.

Simmons, B. (Trans.). (2017). *The Passion Translation: New Testament* (Psalm 127:2 TPT). BroadStreet Publishing.

Simmons, B. (Trans.). (2017). *The Passion Translation: New Testament* (1 Ti 1:18–19). BroadStreet Publishing.

*New American Standard Bible: 1995 update.* (1995). (1 Ti 1:18–19). La Habra, CA: The Lockman Foundation.

Simmons, B. (Trans.). (2017). *The Passion Translation: New Testament* (Psalm 51). BroadStreet Publishing.

*The Holy Bible: English Standard Version.* (2016). (2 Ki 2:19–22). Wheaton, IL: Crossway Bibles.

*The Amplified Bible.* (1987). (Heb 1:14). La Habra, CA: The Lockman Foundation.

# Works Cited

*The Holy Bible: English Standard Version.* (2016). (Ge 1:1–2). Wheaton, IL: Crossway Bibles.

Simmons, B. (Trans.). (2017). *The Passion Translation: New Testament* (Eph 1:3). BroadStreet Publishing.

*The Holy Bible: English Standard Version.* (2016). (Jos 6:26). Wheaton, IL: Crossway Bibles.

*The Holy Bible: English Standard Version.* (2016). (1 Ki 16:33–34). Wheaton, IL: Crossway Bibles.

*The Amplified Bible.* (1987). (1 John 5:14-15). La Habra, CA: The Lockman Foundation.

www.ingramcontent.com/pod-product-compliance
Lightning Source LLC
LaVergne TN
LVHW011838060526
838200LV00054B/4085